The Journey Home

The Journey Home

Written by: Debbie Pierson
Inserts by: Jeffrey Pierson
                       Darrell Pierson.
Edited by: Denise McClaugherty

No part of this publication may be reproduced, stored in a retrieval system or transmitted in any form or by any means without permission.

ISBN-13: 978-0692534656
ISBN-10: 0692534652

Debbie Pierson
28114 Prospect Church Rd.
Mooresboro, NC 28114
Phone: 281-224-2240
Webpage: http://piersons.wix.com/fillmycup
EMAIL: piersondeb@gmail.com

*The ability to maintain strong FAITH
during life's difficulties
is the direct result of having survived
yesterday's storm.*

Preface

A pastor once said "God is not so much concerned about where we end up, but on how we handle the journey." I personally think that there is no need for a journey if it doesn't matter where we end up. It is, however, the experiences from my life's journey that I wish to share with you, and perhaps, through my sharing, your own journey will be a little easier.

Dedication

Darrell Leon Pierson

To the man who has stood by my side.
Never in front, never behind.

I will always love you,
Your devoted wife.

Table of Contents

The Journey	**19**
The Journey Home	20
The Emmaus Road	21
The Long Road Home	23
Family	**27**
Passing the Torch	28
My Sister, My Friend	32
Vinegar Butter	33
A Lifetime of Memories	**37**
Children	38
Jacob	40
A Stone or Bread	41
Dream On	**45**
The Stranger in the Mirror	46
Continue to Dream	47
Just a Whisper	49
Bigger than My Dreams	51
New Seasons	**55**
There is a Time	56
The Changing Seasons	57
The Final Seasons	59
Forever Remember	60
An End and a Beginning	62
Mighty Men of God	**65**
Seth – the anointed Son	66
Joseph	67
Nehemiah	69
Paul	71
Onesimus	73

Peace 77
Eagles Wings 78
Angels 81
Encourage Yourself 85
Awesome God 86
Choose Life 88
Every Knee Shall Bow 90
Trust 92
Forgiveness vs. Trust 94
Healing 96
Prayer 99
Out of My Depth 100
Sleep 101
The Maker of Time 103
A Matter of Time 105
In His Time 107
Calling Into Existence 109
Before The Foundation 112
The Book of James 115
A Made Up Mind 116
Let Me Show You 119
It's all in our mind. 123
The Lion's Roar 124
A Walk with God 126
Forgiven 129
Fulfill Righteousness 131
Godly Influence 134
It's a Spiritual Thing 136
Faith 139
In His Presence 140
Praise the Lord 142

Promises 145
- A Promise, Never Forgotten 146
- He Hears My Prayers 148
- Health and a Long Life 150
- Joy and Peace 152
- A Faithful Friend 154
- Salvation 156
- Sing a New Song 159

The Lord is My Shepherd 163
- I will never want. 164

The Lord's Prayer 167
- Our Father 168
- Our King 170
- Our Provider 171
- Our Deliverer 173

For Generations to Come................................ 177
- All Things Work Together 178
- My Friend 181
- What is an Intercessor? 183
- Outside the Box 186
- Who told? 189
- The Written Word of God 191

Jeffrey Pierson 193
- You Are My Sunshine 194
- Amazing Grace – Part 1 196
- Amazing Grace – Part 2 198
- Amazing Grace – Part 3 200
- Amazing Grace – Part 4 202
- Amazing Grace – Part 5 204
- Faith 207
- Thoughts on Love 211
- Named By God 214

Darrell L Pierson 221
- Thoughts about God 222
- Boots 224
- Mowing the Lawn 227

Teach 233
- Where am I going? 234
- An Opened Door 236
- A Just and Merciful God 237
- Revelation 240
- Not Just For Abraham 242
- A New Year 244
- All Will Know… 252
- Sowing and Reaping 255

Moments to Remember 259
- Angie - August 10, 2008 260
- Christmas 262
- My Comfort Zone 265
- The Water Walker 267
- Water of Life 276
- Thank You 278
- Your Reward 280

The End of the Day 283
- The Trial 284
- The Other Side of Here 287
- Rest 289
- Heaven's Mystery 291
- The Lamb Of God 293
- To God Be the Glory 295

The Journey

When you are unsure of how
to respond, respond in love.

The Journey Home

What is this journey I'm taking?
Where will I find its end?
For as far as my mind remembers,
Picking up, putting down, again.

I know not my destination
Like a pendulum my heart does swing
From rapturous anticipation
To despair of what morning will bring.

Haunted by paths wrongly taken
Fear is the voice in my head
Doubt clouds all my confessions
Endless shadows wherever I tread.

Dreams have ceased to support me
Time has no understanding to lend
I cannot recognize the outcome.
Where will this journey end?

If only someone could teach me
What they know from passing this way
They would whisper the paths old secrets
And peace would fill my day.

Then would I sing the songs of sparrows
I would dance as the angels dance
For knowledge shall drive out all shadows
And wisdom will strengthen my pace.

Come walk with me, sojourner
For you've walked this road before.
You can share the lessons taught you,
And you'll make my heart to soar.

For there are those that you've encountered
On this long journey home
Who walked with you one morning
Having walked this road before.

The Emmaus Road

The Bible tells us about a road that lead from the city of Jerusalem to a town called Emmaus. It was on that road that two men faced the darkest hours of their lives.

Coming from a Jewish background, these men believed that the Messiah would set up His Kingdom on earth allowing the nation of Israel to rule forever.

When Jesus entered the scene all of Israel took notice. Could this be their Messiah? For three and a half years they watched this man heal the sick, cast out devils, restore sight to the blind and cause the deaf to hear. Greatest of all, they saw the dead brought back to life. Surely, no one could do these miracles unless He were the one they waited for.

At the height of Jesus' ministry however, disaster struck and His disciples were left alone, discouraged and frightened. After the burial of their Master, two of these men took the road out of Jerusalem toward Emmaus where they encountered

the risen Christ who revealed to them the eternal hope of God's salvation plan.

Many of us are facing our own dark "Road to Emmaus". We may be one of the millions who have reached the end of the line with no solution to our escalating problems.

Just as the men on the road to Emmaus received hope, we too, can find in God's Word exactly what we need to help us find our way through our own life challenges.

Jeremiah 33:3 (KJV)

Call unto me, and I will answer thee, and shew thee great and mighty things, which thou knowest not.

The Long Road Home

Mark 6:31 (NASV)

And He said to them, "Come away by yourselves to a secluded place and rest a while."

I have often envisioned my life as a long winding road with little cottages at special places along the way. The road represents my life's journey and the days spent traveling on it are full of storms and challenges. But in these little cottages I take refuge from the storm. I lay down the burdens of life for just a little while and regroup for the next leg of my journey toward home.

There is a cord that wanders through the passages of time, defying all who would seek to destroy it.

Impressive and constant, it can neither be broken nor denied.

It is

Family

Ecclesiastes 4:12 (NLT)

A person standing alone can be attacked and defeated, but two can stand back-to-back and conquer. Three are even better, for a triple-braided cord is not easily broken.

Passing the Torch

*Remembering
Shelva Jean Davis Hitchcock.*

James 1:12 (KJV)

Blessed is the man that endureth temptation: for when he is tried, he shall receive the crown of life, which the Lord hath promised to them that love Him.

God granted me a special gift during the winter season of my mother's life. In awe, I witnessed His Word come alive and I will never be the same.

Although mom never acknowledged it, her life was filled with pain and much to my amazement those last days were no different. Yet I feel honored to have witnessed them. I beheld paper transformed into a living, breathing story, all wrapped up in a fragile and delicate gray haired woman, older than her years.

Known for her anointing as a Bible teacher, Mom poured herself into

influencing the lives of others through the lessons she taught. Those last months of her life she taught her final lessons to the students who knew her best, her family.

A favorite story of mine has always been the story of Job and it only gained in popularity during those final days. Her struggle with multiple terminal illnesses never dimmed her faith that God had the power to heal. Heaven's silence would shake, but not deter her. The machine that sustained her breathing echoed words spoken years before:

Job 13:15a (NASV)

"Though He slay me, I will hope in Him."

I caught a glimpse of Peter during those days walking across a raging sea, frightened yet trusting. I saw him the day Mom braced for a life of independence from her husband of fifty years, stumbling under the betrayal of family and friends.

I was touched by the selfless compassion of Steven as I listened to her pray for the healing of a man she hardly knew while quietly accepting her own unanswered prayer.

There was a theme to Moms' lessons and when I am quiet I can hear her whisper from her new home, "It's worth it all."

At Mom's passing the words from Paul to Timothy sealed her life's work, escorting her out of her winter season into eternity.

II Timothy 4:6-8a (KJV)

"For I am now ready to be offered, and the time of my departure is at hand. I have fought a good fight, I have finished my course, I have kept the faith: Henceforth there is laid up for me a crown of righteousness, which the Lord, the righteous judge, shall give me at that day."

There were so many Bible stories that became real to me in this final season, no longer words spoken in a classroom or written in a book but exemplified in the

life of the one I knew so well. Those closing lessons were gifts to me. Now, the torch has passed, the season has changed and I will never be the same.

There was one last lesson Mom taught on what we loving refer to as her "moving day" and this final lesson will carry me home.

1 Corinthians 15:55 (KJV)

"O death, where is thy sting; O grave, where is thy victory"

Romans 8:38-39 (KJV)

For I am persuaded, that neither death, nor life, nor angels, nor principalities, nor powers, nor things present, nor things to come, Nor height, nor depth, nor any other creation, shall be able to separate us from the love of God, which is in Christ Jesus our Lord.

My Sister, My Friend

Ronni

You are God's gift to me. You've taught me that it was okay to laugh, play, sing and live. *(By the way, I'm a slow learner.)*

You have been given a precious gift. The unique ability to "bounce" back from anything life throws at you. I've watched through the years as you've faced many troubles yet your smile continues to shine thru. Thank you for making me question my ability to enjoy life as God intended.

Job 5:26 (NLT)

You will go to the grave at a ripe old age, like a sheaf of grain harvested at the proper time!

Vinegar Butter

I learned from my grandmother how to bake biscuits thick and fluffy. My mother taught me to quilt. My father taught me to take care of my car. My grandfather taught me laughter was contagious. The lessons go on and on. Each person touching my life, leaving behind tidbits of knowledge and I, in turn, pass it on to those that cross my path.

There is a recipe for gravy that my grandmother made. It's called Vinegar Butter. Not everyone has a taste for this unusual dish but I remember it fondly. I don't believe she ever wrote down the recipe but she did teach my mother, who taught me. The gravy is a plum color - IF you know the secret - otherwise, it is colorless and unattractive. I have often wondered if my great grandchildren will have the opportunity to try this treat but unless I teach someone how to make it they will never know.

Our experiences are gifts we can share with future generations. We have a small

window of opportunity to be the giver and when it passes the gifts are lost forever. Many of our experiences as children of God are like my grandmothers gravy. While they remain precious to us and we tenderly embrace the memory, we have not yet shared these gifts with our children.

Pass it on.

Psalm 78:1-7 (NIV)

My people, hear my teaching; listen to the words of my mouth. I will open my mouth with a parable; I will utter hidden things, things from of old— things we have heard and known, things our ancestors have told us. We will not hide them from their descendants; we will tell the next generation the praiseworthy deeds of the Lord, His power, and the wonders He has done. He decreed statutes for Jacob and established the law in Israel, which He commanded our ancestors to teach their children, so the next generation would know them, even the children yet to be born, and they in turn would tell their children. Then they would put their trust in God and would not forget His deeds but would keep His commands.

A Lifetime of Memories

*All of our tomorrows
begin with yesterday's stories.*

Joel 1:3 (NIV)

Tell it to your children, and let your children tell it to their children, and their children to the next generation.

Psalm 127:3 (NLT)

Children are a gift from the LORD; they are a reward from him.

Proverbs 17:6a (NLT)

Grandchildren are the crowning glory of the aged...

Children

1 Samuel 1:27-28a (KJV)

For this child I prayed; and the LORD hath granted me my petition which I asked of Him; therefore I also have given him to the LORD; as long as he liveth he is given to the LORD.

Each day I am reminded of how uncertain this life really is. I listen to the news and I hear of terrorists, disease, and epidemics. I even hear that molesters and murderers are working in the schools. And each day I realize that I have no guarantee that the child I send into this world will return to me - unharmed. What I do have, however, is an assurance that I can trust that my children are in the hands of one who loves them more than I ever could.

When both of my children were just weeks old I gave them back to the Lord. My commitment to Him was that I would do the best I could to teach them His Word, to instill in them integrity and to inspire them to love Him above all else.

Many years have passed since those days. I've made numerous mistakes and often repented to the Lord for the damage I was sure I was inflicting thru my own ignorance. One day while feeling like a complete failure the Lord whispered to me; "Don't you know that I am big enough to cover all your mistakes?" I knew then when I failed God would cover them.

Jacob

Isaiah 49:16a (NIV)

See, I have engraved you on the palms of my hands.

There is a little fellow that has been on my heart this weekend. His name is Jacob. He is new to this world, only a couple of days old. The Bible tells me that my Father in Heaven knows each of us by name. He knows Jacob's name. He sees him and has written his life in a book before he was even conceived. My father sent angels to encamp around Jacob. He is loved not only by his family but heaven has stood by his bedside, watching, caring and overshadowing little Jacob with love. There is something written on the palm of God's hand. It is Jacob. Heaven stands in awe as God Himself smiles upon this one little boy. He is a chosen vessel in the hand of God.

A Stone or Bread

Matthew 7:7-11 (NIV)

"Ask and it will be given to you; seek and you will find; knock and the door will be opened to you. For everyone who asks receives; the one who seeks finds; and to the one who knocks, the door will be opened. Which of you, if your son asks for bread, will give him a stone? Or if he asks for a fish, will give him a snake? If you, then, though you are evil, know how to give good gifts to your children, how much more will your Father in heaven give good gifts to those who ask Him!"

When it comes to my children I am a massive pushover. I have gone into debt up to my eyebrows trying to give them what they wanted. There is a line, however, that I will not cross. That line separates the things that are good for them from the things that will harm them.

Why it that we think God is any different? He is our Father yet somehow we think that His love requires Him to give us everything we ask for. God is love and out of that love He longs to give us our hearts desire; **if** it will not harm us.

Dream On

There are those who say it can't be done, that my dreams are too big and my hopes are too high. They must not know the size of the God I serve.

The Stranger in the Mirror

To my nephew, Christopher Michael Smith. May you forever be at peace with the man in the mirror.

It's the stranger in the mirror
Who tells you who to be
That defines what you believe in
And bows to your defeats

It's the stranger in the mirror
Who sets the course you'll follow,
That reflects on yesterday
Sets values for tomorrow

It's the stranger in the mirror
You know so little of
That will answer for your journey
That's the face that will face God

Continue to Dream

1 Corinthians 15:19 (KJV)

If in this life only we have hope in Christ, we are of all men most miserable.

I have lost many things as I grew older but there is one loss that I was slow to recognize - the ability to dream. I don't mean the kind I do after my eyes shut at night but the ones I dreamed while wide awake. Those dreams have faded as I grew older, consumed by responsibilities, disillusioned by circumstances and I soon discovered the person in the mirror was not the person I thought I should be.

I went in search of my old dreams to discover if they still mattered. Among them I found a few I believe in and I proceeded to set a new course. It's amazing what a dream does for your attitude.

There is one dream I have held on to, however, the dream of meeting my savior

face to face and dwelling with Him for eternity. This dream overshadows all others and makes life worth living.

2 Corinthians 5:1-2 (NIV)

For we know that if the earthly tent we live in is destroyed, we have a building from God, an eternal house in heaven, not built by human hands. Meanwhile we groan, longing to be clothed instead with our heavenly dwelling.

Just a Whisper

Psalm 20:1-4 (NLT)

In times of trouble, may the LORD answer your cry. May the name of the God of Jacob keep you safe from all harm. May He send you help from His sanctuary and strengthen you from Jerusalem. May He remember all your gifts and look favorably on your burnt offerings. May He grant your heart's desires and make all your plans succeed.

Twenty some years ago, as an office assistant, I walked thru the halls of the State Capitol of WV. As I passed the Director of Accounting working at her desk I thought to myself, "Someday I'd like to be the director." I soon forgot that passing dream but little did I know that my Lord recorded my small whisper. Years later I picked up the phone and heard my boss say "As of today you are acting Director of Accounting". I was neither qualified nor was I capable and

the appointment was only temporary. But there was a purpose for this call and I thanked God for this gracious gift. There was another voice I heard that morning, the voice of the Spirit speaking to me – "Remember your whispered dream? I will give you the desires of your heart."

What's Your Dream?

Bigger than My Dreams

Mark 9:23 (KJV)

Jesus said unto him, If thou canst believe, all things are possible to him that believeth.

I was reminded tonight of where I was a few years ago. My life was complete. I would retire in a few years with a decent retirement. I would have a home paid for, money to live on and a good husband to grow old with. I attended a fine church and enjoyed a peaceful relationship with my Lord. Then came the day that the Lord asked me if I was willing to take a chance, to step out of my comfort zone and dare to trust Him. "If you're willing," He said, "I will take you on a journey - but you don't have to go - if you choose not to, it would be just fine, I really won't mind."

I said yes that day, but I really didn't have any idea what I was saying yes to. Now, looking back over these last few years, I am amazed at the wondrous things the Lord has done in my life. I never dreamed

I would ever be in the place I am today with so many opportunities and blessings overtaking me. I never dreamed…But He did…If I had decided not to take a chance, oh the things I would have missed.

Deuteronomy 28:1-6 (NIV)

If you fully obey the Lord your God and carefully follow all His commands I give you today, the Lord your God will set you high above all the nations on earth. All these blessings will come on you and accompany you if you obey the Lord your God: You will be blessed in the city and blessed in the country. The fruit of your womb will be blessed, and the crops of your land and the young of your livestock—the calves of your herds and the lambs of your flocks. Your basket and your kneading trough will be blessed. You will be blessed when you come in and blessed when you go out.

New Seasons

Isaiah 43:18-19 (NAS)

Do not call to mind the former things, Or ponder things of the past. "Behold, I will do something new, Now it will spring forth; Will you not be aware of it? I will even make a roadway in the wilderness, Rivers in the desert.

There is a Time

Ecclesiastes 3 (NIV)

There is a time for everything, and a season for every activity under heavens:

a time to be born and a time to die, a time to plant and a time to uproot,

a time to kill and a time to heal, a time to tear down and a time to build,

a time to weep and a time to laugh, a time to mourn and a time to dance,

a time to scatter stones and a time to gather them, a time to embrace and a time to refrain from bracing,

a time to search and a time to give up, a time to keep and a time to throw away,

a time to tear and a time to mend, a time to be silent and a time to speak,

a time to love and a time to hate, a time for war and a time for peace.

What does the worker gain from his toil? I have seen the burden God has laid on men.

He has made everything beautiful in its time. He has also set eternity in the hearts of men; yet they cannot fathom what God has done from beginning to end.

The Changing Seasons

*Dedicated to my brother, Roger,
who has learned how to wait for the spring.*

Jeremiah 29:11 (NIV)

For I know the plans I have for you," declares the LORD, "plans to prosper you and not to harm you, plans to give you hope and a future.

*Winter whispered a promise
The cold will soon be gone
The hope of sun upon us
Soon we'll be going home.*

I stood behind my mother supporting her as she swayed before the man of God. All eyes were on her hoping that this man could guarantee her healing. "You think that your work for God is over," he said, "but God says He's not finished with you yet."

In the quiet of my soul I knew Mom was only days away from heaven. The Spirit

was not speaking to her but to me and I was the only one who knew it.

Three years later and 1,200 miles away I felt the first glimpse of hope. A forgotten dream was fighting its way into my thoughts. If I could only do something for God before I left this world... if only...

God's timing is not our timing but He remains faithful to carry out His plan at its appointed time. We must simply wait for the season to see that plan fulfilled.

The Final Seasons

It doesn't take mighty deeds to fulfill God's Kingdom's Purpose. It simply takes faithful men and women doing what the Bible says; loving our neighbors, helping the widows and orphans, sowing and reaping. These are just a few of the things we can do so that at the end of the day, when we stand before our Father, He will say,

Matthew 25:21(KJV)

...Well done, thou good and faithful servant: thou hast been faithful over a few things, I will make thee ruler over many things: enter thou into the joy of thy lord.

Forever Remember

Psalm 77:2-6 (NIV)

When I was in distress, I sought the Lord; at night I stretched out untiring hands, and I would not be comforted. I remembered you, God, and I groaned; I meditated, and my spirit grew faint. You kept my eyes from closing; I was too troubled to speak. I thought about the former days, the years of long ago; I remembered my songs in the night..."

As I grow older my mind doesn't seem to work the way it used to. I find myself making notes of anything important because "if it's not written down, it's just not going to happen".

The same principle holds true for my spiritual memory. During the difficult seasons of my life the victories and blessings I've experienced seem to dim or disappear from memory. It takes a decisive effort to bring to mind those experiences but when I do, I am

encouraged as I realize that God has always been there for me and He has never failed me. This current situation will be no different.

Many years ago men and woman kept journals. They would record their thoughts, events and circumstances religiously. Due to the hectic lives people now lead, journals have taken a back seat to daily demands. Wouldn't it be encouraging to have a book that described the many times we've experienced the greatness of God? Wouldn't it be wonderful to read about all the prayers that God has answered? We could pull out our journal and proclaim...

Psalm 77:6 (ESV)

"Let me remember my song in the night; let me meditate in my heart."

An End and a Beginning

I've faced the end of many seasons in my life. There have been times when I grieved for the passing days and other times when I anxiously awaited what lay ahead. The hardest period I have endured, however, is the time spent waiting...waiting for tomorrow, waiting for an answer to prayer, a new job, a child to come home. Amidst the seemingly endless silence there remains a peace for those who wait on the Lord and a strength born from experience.

Psalm 27:14 (KJV)

Wait on the LORD: be of good courage, and He shall strengthen thine heart: wait, I say, on the LORD.

Mighty Men of God

Joshua 1:9 (NASV)

"Have I not commanded you? Be strong and courageous! Do not tremble or be dismayed, for the LORD your God is with you wherever you go."

Seth – the anointed Son

Genesis tells about life "in the beginning". We read of the creation of the earth, moon, sun and stars as well as man and every living creature. We read about the mistakes made in the garden, the punishment for disobedience, even the first murder, when Cain killed his brother, Able. In these pages we also see a new son, Seth, born to Adam and Eve.

This book also records the changing relationship between God and man. We read that God and man were at one time friends, walking together in the cool of the day and we read how that relationship was transformed. The change left man with a deep need to reconnect with God. Today we can enjoy a new era where we can once again walk with God as His friend.

Isaiah 55:6 (NIV)

Seek the LORD while He may be found; call upon Him while He is near.

Joseph

There is a small, inexpensive plaque I gave my mother some 40+ years ago that sits on a shelf in my living room. During that time in her life she experienced many unusual, uncomfortable events, leaving her weary and discouraged. I can still hear her say, "This, too, will pass". The plague reminds me that my mother survived difficult days and it assures me that no matter what I face, tomorrow is just around the corner and if she could do it, so can I.

The Bible tells us the story of a young man who faced many difficult challenges. His name was Joseph. A brother to eleven men, he was rejected, humiliated, falsely accused, imprisoned and separated from those he loved.

Beaten down by circumstances of life, Joseph faithfully trusted that God was in control and would do all that He had promised. For many years Jacob's life was about waiting for dreams to become reality. One day, however, when all that he suffered faded into a memory, Jacob watched his dreams come true. He and his family were reunited.

Acts 7:9-10 (NIV)

Because the patriarchs were jealous of Joseph, they sold him as a slave into Egypt. But God was with him and rescued him from all his troubles. He gave Joseph wisdom and enabled him to gain the goodwill of Pharaoh King of Egypt. So Pharaoh made him ruler over Egypt and all his palace.

When our dreams seem to allude us we must always remember that we are one breath away from our promise.

So breathe!

Nehemiah

The Old Testament is filled with the exploits of the Israelites and the justice of God. The very nature and character of God requires that He reward unrighteousness with justice. Tales of fire falling from heaven, floods covering the earth, or the many plagues that destroyed Egypt have left us with a fear of a God that pronounced such punishments.

While reading Nehemiah, I came across the following passage that brought a new perspective to the God of the Old Testament. Nehemiah spoke of God's mercy and forgiveness, even though he had firsthand knowledge of the judgment of God. Nehemiah faithfully proclaimed that God was patient and longsuffering to His people.

The lesson Nehemiah shared was that of an awesome father who always tempers justice with grace.

Nehemiah 9:17-21 (NLT)

They (the Israelites) refused to obey and did not remember the miracles you (God) had done for them. Instead, they became stubborn and appointed a leader to take them back to their slavery in Egypt! But you are a God of forgiveness, gracious and merciful, slow to become angry, and rich in unfailing love. You did not abandon them, even when they made an idol shaped like a calf and said, 'This is your god who brought you out of Egypt!'... "But in your great mercy you did not abandon them to die in the wilderness. The pillar of cloud still led them forward by day, and the pillar of fire showed them the way through the night. You sent your good Spirit to instruct them, and you did not stop giving them manna from heaven or water for their thirst. For forty years you sustained them in the wilderness, and they lacked nothing. Their clothes did not wear out, and their feet did not swell!

Paul

One of the most well-known figures of the Bible is the Apostle Paul. Having written the majority of the books in the New Testament, he stands out as a World Changer. His exploits include multiple jail visits, beatings, ship wrecks, snake bites and being brought before the high courts, just to name a few. He was a Jewish scholar and a Roman citizen. One of the most educated men of his time. He preached an outstanding message on Mars Hill in the center of the city of Athens proclaiming the 'Unknown God'. He was the catalyst in bringing the Salvation plan to the Gentiles. Yet I found a small reference in Ephesians that shed new light on this powerhouse of a man. Paul wrote to the Ephesians and asked that they pray for him. That wasn't unusual. You'll find similar requests in many of his writings but what stood out to me was what he wanted them to pray for. In this one verse Paul asks for three things.

1. That he would have an appropriate message.
2. That he would be confident when teaching about the gospel.
3. That he would have boldness.

I am reminded through Paul's prayers that all of us face doubts and struggles and just like Paul, we each need to seek help and direction from God.

Ephesians 6:19-20 (NLT)

And pray for me, too. Ask God to give me the right words so I can boldly explain God's mysterious plan that the Good News is for Jews and Gentiles alike. I am in chains now, still preaching this message as God's ambassador. So pray that I will keep on speaking boldly for Him, as I should.

Onesimus

There is a book in the New Testament, written by Paul, to a man known as Philemon. On the surface it seems to be a diplomatic approach to the age old problem of slavery but the truth is, Paul never addressed slavery. Instead, he talked about the responsibility of a child of God to forgive those who have done wrong.

While in prison in Rome, Paul met a runaway slave known as Onesimus who belong to his friend and fellow Christian, Philemon of Colossae. During their time together, Paul led Onesimus to Christ and he grew to love him.

The day came when Onesimus knew he must return to his legal owner and, by law, Philemon had every right to punish him, even to the point of death. With great compassion, Paul writes a letter for Onesimus to take to his master.

In his letter, Paul never denied Onesimus's guilt but he encourages

Philemon to forgive him. He emphasized that they had gained a brother in Christ and he longed to help Philemon accept him as such. Paul concludes by showing his love for both men by offering to pay for all the things Onesimus had wrongfully taken from Philemon.

Philemon's response is not recorded in God's Word but we can only hope that he accepted Onesimus with open arms and counted him as a brother in Christ.

Philemon 1:10-21 (NASV)

I appeal to you for my child Onesimus, whom I have begotten in my imprisonment, who formerly was useless to you, but now is useful both to you and to me. I have sent him back to you in person, that is, sending my very heart, whom I wished to keep with me, so that on your behalf he might minister to me in my imprisonment for the gospel; but without your consent I did not want to do anything, so that your goodness

would not be, in effect, by compulsion but of your own free will. For perhaps he was for this reason separated from you for a while, that you would have him back forever, no longer as a slave, but more than a slave, a beloved brother, especially to me, but how much more to you, both in the flesh and in the Lord.

If then you regard me a partner, accept him as you would me. But if he has wronged you in any way or owes you anything, charge that to my account; I, Paul, am writing this with my own hand, I will repay it (not to mention to you that you owe to me even your own self as well). Yes, brother, let me benefit from you in the Lord; refresh my heart in Christ.

Having confidence in your obedience, I write to you, since I know that you will do even more than what I say.

Peace

*Peace is not a reflection of our circumstances,
for our spiritual nature cannot be touched by natural events.
Peace is a seed
planted by God;
and joy is its harvest.*

Eagles Wings

We are a nation that has enjoyed years of plenty. We have been blessed with abundance to the extent that even the poorest of our families do not compare to those living in 3rd world countries.

Unsuspectingly, a few short months ago, we woke up to a changing world...our world...my world. We found ourselves faced with a series of events that rapidly undermined our well laid plans. The most astonishing thing was that most of us didn't even understand why. All we knew was that a rumble in our financial world resulted in lost jobs, lost businesses, lost homes and lost hope.

We, as Americans, are finding it difficult to "downshift." We are struggling with our limitations; we feel weary in our spirit. Surprisingly this weariness knows no age limit. It is unique in that we can see it in the eyes of those we pass on the street, in the grocery store, or in the car next to us on the freeway. I've seen it in

my own home. It speaks of a weariness that comes from lost dreams.

As I think of our changing world, I am reminded of my Mother's favorite passage. I never understood why she loved it so much but I've concluded her love came from experience. Life exhausted her and robbed her of hope; yet she knew of a secret place where she could find hope once again.

To those of us who are tired of life's challenges I want to encourage you. Wait at the feet of our savior for just a little while. You will learn to fly again.

Isaiah 40:28-31 (NLT)

Have you never heard? Have you never understood? The Lord is the everlasting God, the Creator of all the earth. He never grows weak or weary. No one can measure the depths of His understanding. He gives power to the weak and strength to the powerless. Even youths will become weak and tired, and young men will fall in exhaustion. But those who trust in the Lord will find new strength. They will soar high on wings like eagles. They will run and not grow weary. They will walk and not faint.

Angels

Psalm 34:7 (NIV)

The angel of the LORD encamps around those who fear Him, and He delivers them.

We find images of Angels in art, decorations and numerous other objects. They give us a feeling of safety and comfort, knowing there is someone watching over us. Few of us, however, think about Angels in our everyday life. The Bible tells us that they are all around us.

Hebrews 13:2 (NLT)

Don't forget to show hospitality to strangers, for some who have done this have entertained angels without realizing it!

People often swing to the right or left when it comes to these supernatural beings. They worship them or they deny their existence. For me, I have experienced their help and I give God the Glory. They were a help to Jesus as He walked this earth and I want to be just as willing to accept their help today.

Luke 22:42-43 (NIV)

(Jesus said) "Father, if you are willing, take this cup from me; yet not my will, but yours be done." An angel from heaven appeared to Him and strengthened Him.

Encourage Yourself

1 Samuel 30:6 (KJV)

And David was greatly distressed; for the people spake of stoning him, because the soul of all the people was grieved, every man for his sons and for his daughters: but David encouraged himself in the LORD his God.

Awesome God

Matthew 7:7-11 (NIV)

"Ask and it will be given to you; seek and you will find; knock and the door will be opened to you. For everyone who asks receives; the one who seeks finds; and to the one who knocks, the door will be opened.

"Which of you, if your son asks for bread, will give him a stone? Or if he asks for a fish, will give him a snake? If you, then, though you are evil, know how to give good gifts to your children, how much more will your Father in heaven give good gifts to those who ask Him!

For those of you who know me well, you are aware that there have been many times that I have been greatly challenged in my faith. The illness of my sister, the changes in our ministry, my grandson's life threatening illness, my other grandson's autism and my own health

issues. Many of these challenges have, at times, left me grasping for hope and yet there has been very many other prayers God has answered.

As a testimony to the great God we serve, I thankfully proclaim that God has never failed me. All I have needed His hand has provided and every challenge I faced ultimately proves He is my Sovereign God.

Choose Life

Deuteronomy 30:19-20 (NIV)

This day I call the heavens and the earth as witnesses against you that I have set before you life and death, blessings and curses. Now choose life, so that you and your children may live and that you may love the Lord your God, listen to His voice, and hold fast to Him. For the Lord is your life, and He will give you many years in the land He swore to give to your fathers, Abraham, Isaac and Jacob.

It seems like such an easy choice: life or death. Any of us would readily answer – I choose to live. God promises if we choose life we will be blessed and not cursed. But to choose to live, we must choose Christ.

Each of us will make this choice; yet we are not always conscious of the act of choosing. We choose to serve God or ignore Him. The choice to serve requires a commitment which involves obedience

to His Word. What is your choice? Life or death?

Acts 17:28a (NIV)

For in Him we live and move and have our being.

Every Knee Shall Bow

Psalm 95:6 (KJV)

O come, let us worship and bow down: let us kneel before the LORD our maker.

When is the last time you knelt before the Lord? The position of kneeling shows respect, honor and an attitude of worship.

There will come a day when men and women everywhere will, with one accord, kneel before their creator. On that day there will be no agnostics, atheist or egotistical personalities – the skeptics will believe and all those who called Jesus just a man will behold Him as King of Kings and Lord of Lords.

Philippians 2:10-11 (KJV)

That at the name of Jesus every knee should bow, of things in heaven, and things in earth, and things under the earth; that every tongue should

confess that Jesus Christ is Lord, to the glory of God the Father.

Don't let the judgment seat of God be the next time you kneel before your maker.

Trust

Psalm 56:3 (KJV)

What time I am afraid, I will trust in thee.

There are those who teach that we should never be afraid that true faith in God alleviates all fear. Truthfully, I wish I could say that were true but the reality is that there are days when our circumstances are simply insurmountable. We live in fleshly bodies. We deal with physical situations and often we struggle with our faith.

The psalmist knew exactly what it meant to be afraid. He did not attempt to deny the fear that he felt. Neither did he allow that fear to determine his way of thinking. David made a decision to trust God.

There will be days when we, too, will stagger in fear but we can follow David's example and choose to trust God. And when a simple choice doesn't do the trick,

we can ask our loving Father to help us believe.

Mark 9:24 (KJV)

And straightway the father of the child cried out, and said with tears, Lord, I believe; help thou mine unbelief.

Forgiveness vs. Trust

There is a big difference between forgiving and trusting.

Forgiveness is a command of God and the act of forgiving is the focus. Often, however, we allow unforgiveness to separate us from God and the offense becomes our focus.

Trust, on the other hand, is earned by men/women over time. While it is true that an offense can injure our trust, causing us to be angry and resentful, it is also true that we can choose not to allow it to penetrate our relationship with God by forgiving the offender. But that doesn't mean we trust the offender. Trust must be earned.

Someone who lies to you or deliberately misleads you cannot be trusted. When there is no longer trust, the relationship can no longer be healthy.

Proverbs 12:26a (KJV)

The righteous choose their friends carefully.

Proverbs 9:8 (NIV)

Do not rebuke mockers or they will hate you; rebuke the wise and they will love you.

Healing

Years ago I found myself facing a health crisis. As I began to search Scriptures the healing power of God eluded me and yet I still proclaimed "My God heals." I have been blessed to witness this healing in others but I have not experienced it in my own life. I don't claim to understand. I simply trust God and that is enough.

My sister, however, has been the benefactor of many healings and through them I have found more questions than I have answers; such as, "Why would God heal one part of her body and all the surrounding parts were left diseased?" or "Why would God heal the life threatening infection that resulted from a surgery to rid her of cancer? Why didn't He just heal her of the cancer?"

For many of these questions there are no answers and yet each time I witnessed the selective healing of God in my sister, I am reminded that God still heals today and I maintain the hope that someday He will also heal me.

God has given us many promises in His Word, among them is the promise of health and a long life.

Psalm 118:17 (KJV)

"I shall not die, but live, and declare the works of the LORD."

Prayer

Psalm 56:8 (NLT)

You keep track of all my sorrows. You have collected all my tears in your bottle. You have recorded each one in your book.

Out of My Depth

Proverbs 3:5-6 (NIV)

Trust in the Lord with all your heart and lean not on your own understanding; in all your ways submit to Him, and He will make your paths straight.

Experience is a wonderful teacher but there comes a point when all my experience will not provide me with the direction my circumstances requires. It is at this point I have learned, I **must** hear from God.

*The circumstances' I face today require more than I am equipped to handle.
I turn to God in search of answers. He will direct me.*

Sleep

I read somewhere in a book many years ago and I still remind myself of it on the dark days of life:

> *I will sleep now,*
> *for sleep will take me*
> *a thousand hours*
> *from today.*

At times the events of the day become overwhelming and there is no visible solution. It is then that I refuse to lay awake searching for answers that keep alluding me. I sleep. Rest takes me a thousand hours from today. Perhaps tomorrow I will find the answers that I need.

Psalm 4:8 (NIV)

In peace I will lie down and sleep, for you alone, LORD, make me dwell in safety.

The Maker of Time

Life is not about substance.
It's about breathing, in and
out, day after day.

Acts 17:24-28 (NIV)

"The God who made the world and everything in it is the Lord of heaven and earth and does not live in temples built by human hands. And He is not served by human hands, as if He needed anything. Rather, He Himself gives everyone life and breath and everything else. From one man He made all the nations, that they should inhabit the whole earth; and He marked out their appointed times in history and the boundaries of their lands. God did this so that they would seek Him and perhaps reach out for Him and find Him, though He is not far from any one of us.

'For in Him we live and move and have our being.' As some of your own poets have said, 'We are His offspring.'

A Matter of Time

Genesis 1:14 (NASV)

Then God said, "Let there be lights in the expanse of the heavens to separate the day from the night, and let them be for signs and for seasons and for days and years."

Time is a governing factor for many of us. We organize our lives around it. From a child we measured our existence in days, weeks, and years but when we look into the Word, time is not needed by God. Prior to the creation, about 6,000 years ago, there were no seasons, days, or years....no measurement of time. Time is for this world and is something God created uniquely for us.

In our relationship with God as we seek to know Him better, we must step outside of this fleshly tabernacle into the spiritual realm, for God is a Spirit. We need to see things as God sees them. He is neither burdened nor governed by the limitations of time. When we know that

God has a plan for our lives, we can trust that God will bring all things to pass at the proper time.

Galatians 6:9

Let us not become weary in doing good, for at the proper time we will reap a harvest if we do not give up.

In His Time

The year my daughter turned four I faced a very difficult season. An unexpected, unexplained illness landed her in the hospital and no one could tell me why. Prayers for her life flooded heaven. There is nothing that can make you feel as helpless as a sick child and when your prayers seem to hit a silent God that feeling becomes overwhelming. Early one morning, around 2:00 a.m., I sat by my daughter's bed praying for a miracle; waiting for answers to my endless questions and quickly running out of hope. I became aware of another figure in the room standing at the foot of the bed and I recognized my Lord. Confused, I sensed He was crying. "Lord." I said, "I don't understand. You know what is wrong with her. You know the reason she is sick and you know the outcome; so why are you crying?" Gently he whispered, "Because I also know the pain."

I learned to trust that day... when I didn't understand... and when I wasn't even sure I wanted to. I learned that I didn't need to know how long or when or how God would answer my prayers, I only needed to know He was aware and He loved me. I could rest in knowing He would take care of the rest. In His Time.

Ecclesiastes 3:1 (NLT)

For everything there is a season, a time for every activity under heaven.

Calling Into Existence

Romans 4:17 (NASV)

... God, who gives life to the dead and calls into being that which does not exist.

God stands outside of time. He can see our lives complete from beginning to end because He is not limited to our world. He knows us yesterday, today and tomorrow.

Imagine yourself outside of your body looking at your life played out in front of you. Because of your position you can see clearly the whole picture. You're not stuck in the moment. You could see yourself as a child, as a teenager, on your first date, getting married, or on your first job. That is not a great deal different than when we think back on these same types of things and call it 'a memory'. Imagine, however, that you could also see tomorrow and the day after and the day after that just as clearly as you can see yesterday. You might see a promotion or a new grandbaby. You may even see your retirement or even the end of your life.

It is from this perspective that God views our lives. This is why He calls it done even before it happens. He can see what we can't. He can say, "Congratulations on that new grandbaby" because He sees that child before it is even conceived. Or He can say, "What do you think about that promotion?" when we haven't even gotten the job yet.

When we walk in the spirit we can claim the promises that God has given us in His Word simply because a promise from God can never be denied. It's belongs to us. It's just a matter of Time.

Isaiah 46:9–10 (NASV)

"Remember the former things long past, For I am God, and there is no other; I am God, and there is no one like Me, Declaring the end from the beginning, And from ancient times things which have not been done, Saying, 'My purpose will be established, And I will accomplish all My good pleasure'

Before The Foundation

Psalm 90:2 (NASV)

Before the mountains were born Or You gave birth to the earth and the world, Even from everlasting to everlasting, You are God.

Did we appear out of nothing? Did life just happen by chance? In the depths of all men and women there is a place – deep in our spirit - that acknowledges that there is a Creator. Many will verbally dispute this. Others will block out all knowledge of it. Yet there remains this truth. There is a Creator and He is 'God'.

Before time, before man, before the earth, sun, moon or the stars, there is God. Our minds cannot comprehend His greatness. There is nothing outside of His hand, nothing He cannot control and nothing He does not own. This wonderful, magnificent God is our Creator. We were a thought in the His mind and when that thought was conceived it impregnated the universe and birthed our existence.

Even before anything was created, God new me.

Psalm 139:16 (NLT)

You saw me before I was born. Every day of my life was recorded in your book. Every moment was laid out before a single day had passed.

The Book of James

A Message for all Seasons

The Book of James was written by a man that was quite possibly the Brother of Jesus and the head of the early church. He penned a letter to the churches around 50 A.D. This letter was written under divine inspiration from God Himself. I can imagine our Father whispering, "I've got something so very important I want to share with you and you will need to rehearse it year after year. You will need to keep it before you continually. The best way to do that will be for me to write it down. I will use my willing servant, James, as my transcriber. Listen closely to what I have to say. It is critical for our relationship. It is the key to your joy."

A Made Up Mind

James 1:5-8 (NIV)

If any of you lacks wisdom, you should ask God, who gives generously to all without finding fault, and it will be given to you. But when you ask, you must believe and not doubt, because the one who doubts is like a wave of the sea, blown and tossed by the wind. That person should not expect to receive anything from the Lord. Such a person is double-minded and unstable in all they do.

There is no greater joy for a parent than to give their child what they desire most. At Christmas, when Jeff was a child, he would study the Christmas catalogue intently before he would decide what he wanted most. When he finely showed me the picture of his choice gift, I knew it was exactly what he wanted. Angie, however, would go through the catalogue and mark the pages with comments like, 'I want this' or 'I really want this one'. I was left

to determine among the hundreds of items she chose just which one she might appreciate most. It was the same thing when we went shopping. Angie could be seen pointing to item after item – I want this mom, I want that, while Jeff would just look and maybe see one thing he really wanted.

We are often the same as my daughter when approaching the Lord in prayer. It's not that our Father doesn't desire to give us our hearts request. It's just that we, ourselves, don't know what we really want and we end up asking for things that will mean nothing to us tomorrow. Let's take time today to review our situation and ask for the thing that we truly desire and if our hearts are right, we will find that what we desire is what God desires.

James 4:2-3 (NIV)

You desire but do not have, so you kill. You covet but you cannot get what you want, so you quarrel and fight. You do not have because you do not ask God. When you ask, you do not receive, because you ask with wrong motives, that you may spend what you get on your pleasures.

Let Me Show You

James 2:14-18 (NIV)

What good is it, my brothers and sisters, if someone claims to have faith but has no deeds? Can such faith save them? Suppose a brother or a sister is without clothes and daily food. If one of you says to them, "Go in peace; keep warm and well fed," but does nothing about their physical needs, what good is it? In the same way, faith by itself, if it is not accompanied by action, is dead. But someone will say, "You have faith; I have deeds." Show me your faith without deeds, and I will show you my faith by my deeds.

Our days are filled with opportunities to add works to faith. God places people in our lives with needs that only He can fill and it should be our goal to speak into their life words of hope. When we feel compelled to speak judgment, may we

remember the love He showed us thru the work on Calvary.

When you are unsure of how to respond, respond in love.

It's all in our mind.

Romans 12:2 (NIV)

Do not conform to the pattern of this world, but be transformed by the renewing of your mind. Then you will be able to test and approve what God's will is--his good, pleasing and perfect will.

The Lion's Roar

The Lion is used 92 times in Scripture, often describing circumstances and attitudes, whether good or evil. Because it is used so often, it may be helpful to understand the roar, or method of communication, a Lion uses.

A Lion's Roar:
- intimidates his enemy
- establishes his presence
- proclaims territorial ownership
- communicates with, and rallies, his pride

There is a popular Scripture in Peter that we often quote concerning our enemy, Satan. It contains a warning which tells us to be cautious of the danger Satan can be to an unsuspecting Christian. The fierceness of a Lion is used as a symbol to help us understand.

1 Peter 5:8 (NIV)

Be alert and of sober mind. Your enemy the devil prowls around like a

roaring lion looking for someone to devour.

If we understand the significance of the Roar of a Lion, we can apply this to the Roar of Satan.

Satan's Roar:
- is meant to warn and intimidate us
- establishes his presence in our life
- convinces us that we are in his territory
- communicates with, and rallies, his troops

There is another Scripture, however, that we quote less frequently. It reveals the final spiritual reality that overtakes the terrorizing Roar of Satan.

Revelation 5:5 (NLT)

...Look, the Lion of the tribe of Judah, the heir to David's throne, has won the victory.

A Walk with God

Genesis 3:8-9 (NASV)

They heard the sound of the LORD God walking in the garden in the cool of the day, and the man and his wife hid themselves from the presence of the LORD God among the trees of the garden. Then the LORD God called to the man, and said to him, "Where are you?"

When we consider our day, many of us get up early, get ready for work, wake the kids, fix their breakfast and lunch, get them dressed, rush out the door, deliver them to their designated home-away-from-home, head on to work where we face numerous problems, listen to complaints, answer phones, and deal with bosses. Then we pick up the kids, grab dinner, rush to some after school event, head home, wash some clothes, oversee the homework, bathe the kids and put them in bed.

If you could imagine for one moment, at the end of your day someone waiting for you. You could take an evening walk, watch the sunset, talk about the day and the kids, relax with some tea or coffee and just simply be with the one who cares what you have been going thru during your day.

This is the relationship that Adam and Eve had with God. At the end of the day God would come into the garden to walk and talk with them, just to spend some time with the ones He loved so very much. This close friendship was lost because of disobedience. The remarkable thing is that even amidst the betrayal, guilt, disappointment and the subsequent separation, God immediately let them know that there would be one who would reestablish that relationship. Because of Calvary, we have the privilege of enjoying a walk each God every day.

Take Time to Walk With God

Romans 8:38-39 (KJV)

For I am persuaded, that neither death, nor life, nor angels, nor principalities, nor powers, nor things present, nor things to come, Nor height, nor depth, nor any other creature, shall be able to separate us from the love of God, which is in Christ Jesus our Lord.

Forgiven

Romans 4:7-8 (ESV)

"Blessed are those whose lawless deeds are forgiven, and whose sins are covered; blessed is the man against whom the Lord will not count sin."

There is a season for giving. We call it Christmas. The stores are full of festive lights and holiday decorations. Gifts are exchanged and joy is in abundance. It's the happiest time of the year.

I am reminded of a gift I received a while back. When I received it, I was humbled and overwhelmed. Just thinking of that one gift will bring tears to my eyes even now. The reason this gift was so very special was because it was unexpected, undeserved, unearned and nothing I could ever repay. The most remarkable thing is, the giver didn't even have to do it, he just did, and I needed that gift so very much.

Sometimes we take for granted the special gift we received from God: our salvation. This gift was also unexpected, unearned, and He didn't even have to give it. But God so loved us that He chose to send His own son to provide a way that we all might be reconciled to Him.

I have purposed in my heart this Christmas to give a special gift to someone God lays on my heart. I'd like to challenge you to do the same. Choose someone who is undeserving of any gift from you. Someone who can never give anything back to you. You'll be glad you did. After all, this is what Christmas is all about, giving - without strings.

Matthew 10:8b (NASV)

... Freely you received, freely give.

Fulfill Righteousness

Matthew 3:13-15 (NASV)

Then Jesus arrived from Galilee at the Jordan coming to John, to be baptized by him. But John tried to prevent Him, saying, "I have need to be baptized by You, and do You come to me?" But Jesus answering said to him, "Permit it at this time; for in this way it is fitting for us to fulfill all righteousness." Then he permitted Him.

In our quest to know the will of God in our lives we search Scripture, intent on understanding the truths buried in the pages. While seeking knowledge, however, it is important for us to begin with a clear grasp of the message Jesus gave us in the Gospels; Matthew, Mark, Luke, and John. It is in these books that we learn the basics for our walk with God.

Water baptism is one of those basics and it is directly related to our new birth in Christ. There are a variety of ways men practice this ordinance. Some feel it is the very act of immersing in water that cleanses us from sin. Others feel it does not require immersion but the sprinkling of water to sufficiently fulfill Christ commands. Still others interpret it as an outward statement of an inward change in their life. Whatever our current understanding is of the process, we can rest assured that Jesus fulfilled every part of the righteous law of God and that simple truth is, Jesus was baptized. What is hindering us from doing likewise?

Acts 8:35-38 (NASV)

The eunuch answered Philip and said, "Please tell me, of whom does the prophet say this? Of himself or of someone else?" Then Philip opened his mouth, and beginning from this Scripture he preached Jesus to him. As they went along the road they came to some water; and the eunuch said, "Look! Water! What prevents me from being baptized?" [And Philip said, "If you believe with all your heart, you may." And he answered and said, "I believe that Jesus Christ is the Son of God."] And he ordered the chariot to stop; and they both went down into the water, Philip as well as the eunuch, and he baptized him.

Godly Influence

Psalm 1:1-2 (NASV)

How blessed is the man who does not walk in the counsel of the wicked, Nor stand in the path of sinners, Nor sit in the seat of scoffers! But his delight is in the law of the LORD, And in His law he meditates day and night.

I have sought advice from many during times of crises. Hurt, confused and floundering, I've placed my trust in well-meaning people, seeking righteous direction only to find their wisdom did not reflect the heart of God. Experience and Biblical knowledge has taught me to seek a chosen few to speak to in my life. Those selective few have earned that right through the years of proven stewardship.

The Psalmist gave guidelines regarding those we allow to influence us. He states:

1. Avoid seeking advice of someone who does not have a relationship with God.

They walk thru life without spiritual influence and their guidance will reflect that void.

2. Do not walk with those who disagree with God's laws. Their life is full of sinful deeds and their influence will lead you to a comfortable acceptance of sin in your own life.

3. Never sit down with one who scorns righteousness. Those individuals have set their course for eternity and their commitment to unrighteousness is transmittable.

The Psalmist concludes with one simple directive. Know the Word of God and take pleasure in obeying it.

It's a Spiritual Thing

John 4:23-24 (NASV)

But an hour is coming, and now is, when the true worshipers will worship the Father in spirit and truth; for such people the Father seeks to be His worshipers. "God is spirit, and those who worship Him must worship in spirit and truth."

To understand that God is our creator, we must first recognize God in our 'spirit'. We cannot recognize Him in the 'natural' because you cannot feel, touch, smell, or taste God. You cannot recognize Him in you 'soul' or intellect because He cannot be explained, rationalized or conceptually proven. Your feelings will mislead you for they often have no frame of reference to draw from. For you to acknowledge there is a God, it requires your 'spirit' to recognize Him. It is in your 'spirit' that you know He exists.

Faith

*We cannot even begin
to manifest our faith
until the circumstances
we face are hopeless
and Heaven is silent.*

Psalm 141:1–2

I call to you, Lord, come quickly to me; hear me when I call to You. May my prayer be set before You like incense; may the lifting up of my hands be like the evening sacrifice.

In His Presence

Psalm 42:1-2 (NIV)

As the deer pants for streams of water, so my soul pants for You, my God. My soul thirsts for God, for the living God. When can I go and meet with God?

There is a place I love to visit – it is the place of God's presence and it is there that I am transformed.

Many years ago I found myself emotionally, mentally and physically spent. Life had depleted me of all my strength. One evening I knelt beside my bed and prayed a simple, but desperate, prayer. "God, I can't do this. If it's going to be done, you'll have to give me strength." With that one sentence hanging in the air, I pulled myself into bed and fell into a deep sleep. Hours later, before I opened my eyes, I felt that something had changed.

Matthew 4:11b (NASV)

... behold, angels came and began to minister....

I knew instantly that God had sent His Angels to minister to me. I felt equipped to handle what was before me.

I have had many such experiences during my walk with God. Each one has been unique and life changing. A simple word from God will turn my night to day, and today I cry out "Lord, do it again."

Praise the Lord

Praise means to shine, to make a show; to boast; and to be (clamorously) foolish; to rave; to celebrate.

I love to feel the presence of the Lord. It fires my emotions and overwhelms me with gratitude, awe and humility. I find it easy to praise God when I feel Him near yet I have learned thru the years that I cannot wait for emotions to stir up my praise. The praise God treasures most from me is not the reaction to His touch - but it is the praise I give Him when I don't FEEL like praising. This type of praise does not have to wait for the moment but it is birthed out of the knowledge that God is worthy.

*Praise is an Action
not a reaction.*

Psalm 150:1-6 (NASV)

Praise the LORD!

Praise God in His sanctuary;

Praise Him in His mighty expanse.

Praise Him for His mighty deeds;

Praise Him according to His excellent greatness.

Praise Him with trumpet sound;

Praise Him with harp and lyre.

Praise Him with timbrel and dancing;

Praise Him with loud cymbals;

Let everything that has breath praise the LORD.

Praise the LORD!

Promises

Numbers 23:19 (NIV)

God is not human, that He should lie, not a human being, that He should change his mind. Does He speak and then not act? Does He promise and not fulfill?

A Promise, Never Forgotten

Have you ever made a promise you could not keep, or told someone something you had to take back? Keeping my word has always been a priority yet I have found myself in a quandary at times – unable to follow thru on what I promised I would do.

When God makes a promise, however, there can be no dilemma; there will never be 'unusual circumstances.' What God says will come to pass because when He 'speaks' there is no excuse for it not happening. A record of God's many promises can be found in the Bible.

Abram was a man that God made many promises to. One of those promises was that he would have a child and from that child, a nation would be. So great a nation that no one would be able to count them. Isaac was that child.

A thousand years after Abram, a man called Moses looked across a multitude of people known as the Israelite nation and

remembered the promise God had made to Abraham.

Deuteronomy 1:10-11 (NIV)

The Lord your God has increased your numbers so that today you are as numerous as the stars in the sky. May the Lord, the God of your ancestors, increase you a thousand times and bless you as He has promised!

He Hears My Prayers

Jeremiah 29:12-13

Then you will call on me and come and pray to me, and I will listen to you. You will seek me and find me when you seek me with all your heart.

The greatest struggle a Christian faces is prayer. We cannot understand how the maker of all things could care about us or that He would hear what we say.

As early as the Garden of Eden, Satan tried to separate man and God by telling Adam that God was withholding good things from him *(the fruit from the tree of Knowledge)* for His own selfish reasons. This original lie became a road block between mankind and God, crippling our ability to talk with Him and causing us to doubt that He really cares for us.

However, God loves us as a Father loves his son. He cares for us so much that He tore down the wall that separated us from His presence and He encouraged us to

meet with Him once again, promising that He will always hear us when we pray.

1 John 5:14-15 (NIV)

This is the confidence we have in approaching God: that if we ask anything according to His will, He hears us. And if we know that He hears us - whatever we ask - we know that we have what we asked of Him.

Health and a Long Life

Exodus 15:26 (NLT)

He said, "If you will listen carefully to the voice of the LORD your God and do what is right in His sight, obeying His commands and keeping all His decrees, then I will not make you suffer any of the diseases I sent on the Egyptians; for I am the LORD who heals you."

When I consider Jesus and His time on earth, I am overwhelmed at what He accomplished during those short 3 ½ years of ministry. His purpose was to bring salvation to the world by restoring man's relationship with God. With such a great responsibility on His shoulders, Jesus still took time to heal the sick. He cares about us when we are sick. He cares about me when I am sick.

After watching "The Passion", I was moved in my spirit at the reality of what Jesus faced. Speechless, I walked to the restroom where an unusual silence

hovered in the room. There was one thought that echoed in my head, "Why wouldn't He heal me? "

1 Peter 2:24 (ESV)

He Himself bore our sins in His body on the tree, that we might die to sin and live to righteousness. By His wounds you have been healed.

Joy and Peace

I've been privileged to make the acquaintance of many 'characters' during my life. Some have impacted my spiritual growth more than others. They are not necessarily the popular or wealthy, the talented or productive but they have a presence about them that draws me into their camp. They have faced fire, flood and wind yet their faith remains unmovable and their attitude positive. They have an undeniable atmosphere about them; one that is filled with peace.

Peace cannot be explained. We can't handle it and we can't intellectually rationalize its existence. Peace is borne in our spirit; a gift from God. Peace will take us thru the dark days of life. It will calm us in our most fearsome storm. Ultimately, it will produce Joy unspeakable.

John 14:27

Peace I leave with you; my peace I give to you. Not as the world gives do I give to you. Let not your hearts be troubled, neither let them be afraid.

John 16:33

These things I have spoken unto you, that in me ye might have peace. In the world ye shall have tribulation: but be of good cheer; I have overcome the world.

A Faithful Friend

1 Thessalonians 5:24 (ESV)

He who calls you is faithful; He will surely do it.

JEHOVAH-JIREH - "The Lord will Provide."

Isaiah 40: 28–31 (NASV)

Do you not know? Have you not heard? The Everlasting God, the LORD, the Creator of the ends of the earth does not become weary or tired. His understanding is inscrutable. He gives strength to the weary, And to him who lacks might He increases power. Though youths grow weary and tired, And vigorous young men stumble badly, Yet those who wait for the LORD Will gain new strength; They will mount up with wings like eagles, They will run and not get tired, They will walk and not become weary.

The majority of my life I have faced minimal opposition. However, there have been the inevitable days when life simply slams me. It's in those times that I feel overwhelmed and exhausted. Not only mentally and emotionally, but also spiritually. It's in the middle of those situations that I just want to quit. I have no idea how I could possibly cease what I'm going through but the feeling of wanting to is definitely there.

I have lived many years for the Lord and there have been many times I witnessed His mercy and His help. These experiences taught me that I won't always feel the way I feel now. There will come a day when I will walk away from this storm and if I just hold on to God, I'll make it through. In fact, I may just be one heartbeat away from my victory. I have, on many occasions, seen my whole life change in just one breath. My greatest challenge is to wait on the Lord.

Salvation

Ephesians 2:4-9 (NASV)

But God, being rich in mercy, because of His great love with which He loved us, even when we were dead in our transgressions, made us alive together with Christ (by grace you have been saved), and raised us up with Him, and seated us with Him in the heavenly places in Christ Jesus, so that in the ages to come He might show the surpassing riches of His grace in kindness toward us in Christ Jesus. For by grace you have been saved through faith; and that not of yourselves, it is the gift of God; not as a result of works, so that no one may boast.

In the Garden of Eden the Bible says that God walked in the cool of the day looking for Adam **(Genesis 3:8)**. Adam and God were good friends. God never intended, however, to force this relationship so He gave Adam a precious gift. The right to

choose to remain in a relationship with Him or to pull away in disobedience.

Adam's rebellion against God came about when he ate from the Tree of Knowledge that God had instructed him to leave alone. The result was that sin corrupted his heart and his disobedience destroyed their fellowship because righteousness can never keep company with unrighteousness.

The greatest promise mankind ever received was given on that dark day in history. God promised that He would send a Savior that would restore their injured relationship but the restoration would not come easy. There would be a cost. A sacrifice must be made to cover the sin of man and wash him clean. Jesus was that sacrifice and today the price is paid in full removing every barrier between us and God. There remains one last thing that we must do to be brought back into fellowship with God. Each of us must choose, just as Adam chose.

Romans 10:9 (NLT)

If you confess with your mouth that Jesus is Lord and believe in your heart that God raised him from the dead, you will be saved.

John 3:16-18 (NIV)

For God so loved the world that he gave his one and only Son, that whoever believes in him shall not perish but have eternal life. For God did not send his Son into the world to condemn the world, but to save the world through him. Whoever believes in him is not condemned, but whoever does not believe stands condemned already because they have not believed in the name of God's one and only Son.

Sing a New Song

Psalm 68:3-5 (NLT)

But let the godly rejoice. Let them be glad in God's presence. Let them be filled with joy. Sing praises to God and to His name! Sing loud praises to Him who rides the clouds. His name is the LORD - rejoice in His presence! Father to the fatherless, defender of widows - this is God, whose dwelling is holy.

People cherish memories from childhood that relate to vacation, Christmas morning or some other special events. For me, I remember singing. Christian music has been a part of my life for as long as I can remember. Holidays inevitably found us gathered around the kitchen table with my grandfather and his guitar leading the family in all our favorite tunes. He would lead us into worship and the room would fill with God's presence.

There is nothing like a song to lift my spirits. As a teenager I would embarrass my younger sister by bellowing out songs while we shopped in Krogers. She would dart to another isle, pretending she didn't know me.

There was so much joy in my soul and rejoicing in my spirit that I just had to sing. My joy from singing, however, had nothing to do with my ability. When my son was young he would say, "Please mommy, don't sing". I never knew if it was the song or the sound that disturbed him most.

Storms and struggles of life have at times silenced my song - for a season. Thankfully, all seasons pass and the morning would come. I would wake up and once again I would hear a song - deep in my spirit, embracing me like a long lost friend.

The Lord is My Shepherd

Everyone faces dark days in their life. They are filled with the death of a parent, the betrayal of a friend, the end of a marriage, the loss of a child. Events play out in our life while we struggle to find our way to the other side of grief. This passage found in Psalm is one of the most well-known and speaks to the broken hearted.

I will never want.

Psalm 23:1 (NIV)

The LORD is my shepherd, I lack nothing.

"The Lord is my shepherd" portrays a guardian who is watching over us; one who cares about us as a shepherd cares for his flock. "I shall not want" reminds us that our shepherd accepts the responsibility for supplying all our needs.

I met Jesus many years ago and invited Him to be a part of my life. Today I call Him Lord, my Redeemer, my Healer and my Friend. But there is no truer description then that of "Shepherd". I think Isaiah says it best.

Isaiah 40:11 (NIV)

He tends His flock like a shepherd: He gathers the lambs in His arms and carries them close to His heart; He gently leads those that have young.

The Lord's Prayer

When the disciples came to Jesus asking how they ought to pray, He gave them an example. We call it "The Lord's Prayer". This prayer, like so many passages in the Bible, teaches us principles that we need to understand when we approach God. It is not merely the utterance of words that draws God's attention but the "protocol" of our prayer.

Our Father

Matthew 6:9 (NASV)

"Pray, then, in this way: "Our Father who is in heaven, Hallowed be Your name.

Jesus began His lesson with the following two, often overlooked, principles and yet they are key elements in approaching God. Unless we can grab hold of these truths, we will walk away from our time in prayer feeling as if we were talking to a wall.

1. We must have a clear understanding of our relationship with God, He is our Father.
2. We must maintain an attitude of Honor toward Him.

It is difficult for those who have a poor example of a father - or who have never known one - to relate to God in this role. Many do not even know what a father's role is. Our culture teaches us that we need to honor no one but our self. So for

us to honor God requires that we understand that He is worthy of our honor.

It is these barriers that we must overcome so that we can align our beliefs to the truth of God's Word. Only when we believe God's Word can we begin to communicate with Him in prayer.

Our King

Matthew 6:10 (NASV)

'Your kingdom come. Your will be done, On earth as it is in heaven.

My early understanding of the workings of God was often influenced by good intended, unlearned Biblical teachers. Their teachings clouded the reality of God's love for me. I assumed that for me to be accepted by God I had to be in His perfect will - always. I was convinced that God would force me into submission to His will or I would burn in Hell.

Through the years I learned about the Love of God and that He would not easily reject me. I also realized that when I failed to find, or follow, His will in my life, He continue to love me. He patiently guided me in the direction that He knew was best for me. I discovered that it gave God great joy when I followed His will; much like a father takes pride in the obedience of his own child. Now I eagerly say, "Your will, and not mine be done."

Our Provider

Matthew 6:11 (NASV)

'Give us this day our daily bread.

In today's world it is easy to be overcome with fear when we realize how little control people have over their own destiny. A lost job, a health crisis, even a broken down vehicle can raise panic. Our needs lay at the mercy of bosses, governments and sometimes family and friends. If they don't help us, who will?

There are many such circumstances all around us, every day. Sometimes the needs are our own, sometimes they belong to others we know and love.

We have a promise. God sees our needs and He cares. We only have to ask .... and believe He hears and answers.

Matthew 6:25-26 (NIV)

"Therefore I tell you, do not worry about your life, what you will eat or drink; or about your body, what you will wear. Is not life more than food, and the body more than clothes? Look at the birds of the air; they do not sow or reap or store away in barns, and yet your heavenly Father feeds them. Are you not much more valuable than they?

Our Deliverer

Matthew 6:13 (NASV)

And do not lead us into temptation, but deliver us from evil. [For Yours is the kingdom and the power and the glory forever. Amen.']

In my life I have been continually surprise by the evil things that men and women do. There are times when their actions touch my life and I am on the front line witnessing the consequences of their sins.

Evil may surround me but I have a hiding place in God. I run to my Father and He sets a camp of protection around me. He will place me in His pavilion and I will find rest.

Psalm 27:4-5 (KJV 2000)

One thing have I desired of the LORD, that will I seek after; that I may dwell in the house of the LORD all the days of my life, to behold the beauty of the LORD, and to inquire in His temple. For in the time of trouble He shall hide me in His pavilion: in the secret place of His tabernacle shall he hide me; He shall set me up upon a rock.

For Generations to Come

3 John 1:4

I have no greater joy than to hear that my children are walking in the truth.

All Things Work Together

Romans 8:27-29 (NLT)

And the Holy Spirit helps us in our weakness. For example, we don't know what God wants us to pray for. But the Holy Spirit prays for us with groanings that cannot be expressed in words. And we know that God causes everything to work together for the good of those who love God and are called according to His purpose for them. For God knew His people in advance, and He chose them to become like His Son, so that His Son would be the firstborn, with many brothers and sisters.

There have been many storms in my life, each one proving to me that My God works all things together for my good.

Storms are those times when we are surrounded by circumstances and events that we have no power to change. We easily become overwhelmed with the hopelessness of our situation. And yet, no

matter how hard it has been, I can see the hand of God through each of those experiences. I have grown stronger in faith and with each new storm I am less intimidated than I was with the one before.

There was one particular storm that knocked the wind out of my sails and it took me about a year to find my balance. Thru that storm many things changed. My goals, my dreams, my intents; they all took a turn in a new direction. At the end, I ask God why I had to walk through this time in my life. His reply was simple. "I allowed this storm in your life because you could not hear my direction."

I had a plan, I had a goal, and I had set my course. There was nothing wrong with these plans or the place I intended to go but I was so intent on reaching my destination I could not hear the voice of God urging me to change course.

It was then that a storm came into my life, tossing me about until I lost all sense of direction. I was confused and lost. But when the winds died down and the storm passed, I had to set a new course. One that God had intended all along.

Now I try to look at each challenge as an opportunity to find God's direction, His help, and His love. I make an effort to keep my mind opened to what changes this storm will bring to my life – for God will ultimately bring it together for my good.

My Friend

Job 1:19-21

Even now my witness is in heaven; my advocate is on high. My intercessor is my friend as my eyes pour out tears to God; and He contends with God on behalf of man as a man pleads for his friend.

Every class room has a bully and a victim. In grade school I found myself living the life of the victim. The 'class' system left me feeling alone and defenseless. Even today I find I still need an intercessor but it isn't people that I fear but the righteous judgment of God.

Matthew 10:28 (NIV)

Do not be afraid of those who kill the body but cannot kill the soul. Rather, be afraid of the One who can destroy both soul and body in hell.

I am grateful that Jesus has taking up my cause and intercedes for me. I have nothing to fear. I cannot be condemned for He calls me His friend.

Romans 8:34 (KJV)

Who is he that condemneth? It is Christ that died, yea rather, that is risen again, who is even at the right hand of God, who also maketh intercession for us.

What is an Intercessor?

Intercede means to make an earnest request or petition to God on behalf of another.

The phrase 'intercessory prayer' is often frightening for many Christians. We have reserved the position of an intercessor for someone who spends a great deal of time in their prayer closet. A person who hears awesome truths from God or the person WE go to when we need an answer to our prayers.

What is an intercessor?

- As an intercessor you should know the person you are interceding for.
- As an intercessor you must be in a relationship (connected) to God.
- As an intercessor you must come before God with reverence (a feeling of awe and respect) and an attitude of worship (of love and devotion, often expressed in song or prayer).

- As an intercessor you do not seek recognition for your role in the process.
- As an intercessor you must recognize that you are not the decision maker. It is not your responsibility to decide what the best and final course of action is. It is your responsibility to present the request to God.
- As an intercessor you must trust the sovereignty of God, believing that He will act according to His purpose and plan.
- As an intercessor you must persist until the petition has been acted on.
- As an intercessor you must know when to allow the Spirit to pray through you.

Romans 8:26-27 (NLT)

And the Holy Spirit helps us in our weakness. For example, we don't know what God wants us to pray for. But the Holy Spirit prays for us with groanings that cannot be expressed in words. And the Father who knows all hearts knows what the Spirit is saying, for the Spirit pleads for us believers in harmony with God's own will.

Outside the Box

Proverbs 19:21 (ESV)

Many are the plans in the mind of a man, but it is the purpose of the Lord that will stand.

For many of us, the only legacy we will ever leave behind is a long list of unfulfilled dreams, remnants of what we had hoped was God's purpose and will for our life. All too often we search through the rubble of yesterday, looking for that one dream that might become today's reality.

Can we really know God's plan for our life? Even though we long to know the will of God, we find ourselves doing the next thing that crosses our path simply because it needs to be done and we don't know what else to do. The result is feelings of disillusionment, frustration and exhaustion, yet we keep 'beating the air' in an effort to accomplish something for our Savior.

We often seek clarity among the predefined roles that are set in place by well-meaning organizations that were formed by men and women who were seeking the purpose and plan of God in their own world. These roles are important to operate in excellence while we are on this earth but I fear we are losing our ability to hear from God on a personal level.

If we would step away from the expectations of these predefined roles and take a fresh look at what the Word of God says concerning His purpose and plan, we will find His will. There are many times God places us in the very same roles that have been set in place by our churches but then there are times that God longs for us to operate outside of the box. Outside of a position or title so that His own unique purpose will play out in our life.

God's purpose always produces peace of mind and a deep rooted sense of fulfillment and it will give birth to our finest hour. While it can be challenging, His purpose will not be grievous.

Matthew 11:28-30 (NASV)

"Come to Me, all who are weary and heavy-laden, and I will give you rest. Take My yoke upon you and learn from Me, for I am gentle and humble in heart, and you will find rest for your souls. For My yoke is easy and My burden is light."

Who told?

One of the great stories of all times is the Story of Creation. Who was it that heard it first? No human was present to behold those wondrous works of God. Those magnificent and breathtaking events could only be told to us by the Creator Himself. And how does the Creator explain in human terms what wonders took place so long ago?

We know that the Glory of God was evident when "nothing" became a mass of water, and water moved aside to allow dry land to appear. If we could only visualize the moment when the sun was spoken into existence. The Angels saw and 'shouted for joy.'

Job 38:4-7 (NIV)

"Where were you when I laid the earth's foundation? Tell me, if you understand. Who marked off its dimensions? Surely you know! Who stretched a measuring line across it? On what were its footings set, or who

laid its cornerstone—while the morning stars sang together and all the angels shouted for joy?

I can only hope that there is a record in Heaven of the events that took place that day so that, with our own eyes, we can see the wonders of those first days of creation. Yet we find a greater than this promised...

1 Corinthians 2:9 (KJV)

But as it is written, Eye hath not seen, nor ear heard, neither have entered into the heart of man, the things which God hath prepared for them that love him.

The Written Word of God

We find in God's Word that our Father tells us to seek wisdom and understanding. But where can we find it? How do we know what God would have us do? When will He tell us?

God will not hide the answers to our questions from us like a sadistic God who takes pleasure in our ignorance and confusion. But He freely offers us a clear revelation of His plan and purpose in the pages of His Written Word.

Proverbs 2:1-5 (NIV)

My son, if you accept my words and store up my commands within you, turning your ear to wisdom and applying your heart to understanding—indeed, if you call out for insight and cry aloud for understanding, and if you look for it as for silver and search for it as for hidden treasure, then you will understand the fear of the Lord and find the knowledge of God

Jeffrey Pierson

Proverbs 23:24 (NLT)

The father of godly children has cause for joy. What a pleasure to have children who are wise.

You Are My Sunshine

By Debbie Pierson

You Are My Sunshine
Written Jimmie Davis and Charles Mitchell
Copyright 1940 and 1977 by Peer International Corporation.

> You Are My Sunshine
> My only sunshine.
> You make me happy
> When skies are grey.
> You'll never know, dear,
> How much I love you.
> Please don't take my sunshine away.

The simple words of the song never fails to bring a smile. I remember clearly a bright sunny day in the mountains of WV, driving down the road with my infant son by my side, singing to him and thanking God for his happy nature. My daughter's 1st months of life were full of colic and sleepless nights. A new mother, with no experience or confidence, I had not wanted to go through that experience

again and dreaded those first months of an unexpected 2nd pregnancy.

Jeffrey Lee Pierson entered this world in a rush. All 10 lbs. of him arrived less than 30 minutes after we arrived at the hospital. Recovery was much easier the second time around and with no sign of colic, we quickly settled into a comfortable schedule. He seldom complained unless he was hungry.

Little did I know this happy little boy's life would be full of challenges I would never understand. But in those first days of life, I will never forget the sunshine he brought to me.

Amazing Grace – Part 1

Jeffrey Pierson - January, 2010

*Amazing Grace, how sweet the sound,
That saved a wretch like me.
I once was lost but now am found,
Was blind, but now I see.*

By John Newton
Composed between 1760 and 1770

We often forget the beautiful sound of Grace. Before we were saved we did terrible things and hurt many people without even realizing it. We were hopeless and afraid and most of us, myself included, couldn't even see it. We didn't know where to turn and most of us didn't even know that we were going the wrong way.

Then one day a light shined into our dark lives and lit the path we were on. We saw the end of our road and knew death and loneliness awaited. From the light shining on our backs we heard a voice crying out, "Come to me and be forgiven." Many of us replied, "I can't. I have nothing to give you. My life is worthless

and I have hurt so many people." "Come to me," Said the voice. "All your sins were against me and me alone. All your debts are to me and I forgive them freely."

In all my life I have never found a more beautiful sound than this.

2 Corinthians 4:3-4 (KJV)

But if our gospel be hid, it is hid to them that are lost: In whom the god of this world hath blinded the minds of them which believe not, lest the light of the glorious gospel of Christ, who is the image of God, should shine unto them.

Amazing Grace – Part 2

Jeffrey Pierson - January, 2010

*T'was Grace that taught my heart to fear.
And Grace, my fears relieved.
How precious did that Grace appear
The hour I first believed.*

By John Newton
Composed between 1760 and 1770

I remember when I first discovered that God and hell were both real. When I was a child my foot was broken and had healed a little off. By the time I was in college the condition of my foot had deteriorated to the point that I walked with a cane most of the time. One day I had several people pray for my foot because it was expected of a good man of the church. I got up without pain and walked back to my seat with no trace of a limp. It was then that I realized that God was interested in my life.

It was several days before I began to think about the implications of a God who was paying attention to me. When I began to think about the things I had done I was

terrified. How could I ever face a God who was perfect and holy and expected me to be holy and righteous just like He was. For the first time in my life I knew true fear as the prospect of an unending torment and separation from my loved ones stretched out before me. I fell on my knees and begged for forgiveness only to have God whisper in my ear, "It was always yours for the asking. You are My son and I have always loved you."

I clung to that precious grace as if it were all the gold in the world and yet even this comparison pales next to the true value of this gift.

Proverbs 19:23 (NLT)

Fear of the Lord leads to life, bringing security and protection from harm.

Amazing Grace - Part 3

Jeffrey Pierson - January, 2010

Through many dangers, toils and snares
I have already come;
'Tis Grace that brought me safe thus far
and Grace will lead me home.

By John Newton
Composed between 1760 and 1770

Since the day I gave my life to Christ I have never looked back. Many times I have fallen, been afraid and even been blinded by pride and blatantly sinned thinking that I knew God better than the people that taught me of Him. Yet every time I go astray I can hear His voice calling me back. I have faced times when my heart was broken and I could see no way out of the horrors around me yet His Spirit never let me falter and filled me with the strength to travel on. And in the most trying time of my life, when all I wanted to do was grieve the loss of my grandmother and hate both the man who abandoned her at the end and the doctors who had prescribed the medicine that

devastated her health, all He would let me feel was joy at her passing into His presence and true grief at the plight of those who hurt His children.

I may not be very old, but I have lived long enough to know that no matter what awaits me in the days to come if I hold tight to my God, He will not let me fail before I make it home.

1 Corinthians 10:13 (KJV)

There hath no temptation taken you but such as is common to man: but God is faithful, who will not suffer you to be tempted above that ye are able; but will with the temptation also make a way to escape, that ye may be able to bear it

Amazing Grace – Part 4

Jeffrey Pierson - January, 2010

The Lord has promised good to me.
His word my hope secures.
He will my shield and portion be,
As long as life endures.

By John Newton
Composed between 1760 and 1770

How often do we forget what God has promised? I had a revelation today. God chastised me for focusing on the promises I have not seen revealed yet, when he has done so much already. I looked back on my life and realized that much of what I saw as a lack of anything happening was actually God shielding me from this world. And when I saw only a lack of the things I thought I needed, I failed to notice that I was still living and even thriving.

We often look at our lives as a testament to how much we need God and forget that sometimes the greatest of His promises are just to help us through the day. God has made many great promises to me

over the years but most are for the future. Today he has promised me peace and joy and rest and I can accept them until He decides it is time for everything else.

Isaiah 40:31 (KJV)

But they that wait upon the LORD shall renew their strength; they shall mount up with wings as eagles; they shall run, and not be weary; and they shall walk, and not faint.

Amazing Grace - Part 5

Jeffrey Pierson - January, 2010

Yea, when this flesh and heart shall fail, and mortal life shall cease, I shall possess within the veil, a life of joy and peace. When we've been here ten thousand years bright shining as the sun. We've no less days to sing God's praise than when we've first begun.

By John Newton
Composed between 1760 and 1770

When my Grandmother died I was filled with grief for a few days but that grief passed quickly into a faded memory. Later when my Grandfather passed away I had comfort knowing that he had accepted God in the end. We are eternal beings forged by God himself to be indestructible yet we cannot see past the boundaries of our mortality. We often see death as an end, a thick curtain at the edge of the room and when someone steps through they are gone and we know not where. The greatest gift that God has given us is not the few short years we have in this world but the promise that if

we follow Him we will step through that curtain into our true life which will never end and will not be tarnished by the pain and turmoil we face in this world.

1 Thessalonians 4:13-18 (KJV)

But I would not have you to be ignorant, brethren, concerning them which are asleep, that ye sorrow not, even as others which have no hope. For if we believe that Jesus died and rose again, even so them also which sleep in Jesus will God bring with him. For this we say unto you by the word of the Lord, that we which are alive and remain unto the coming of the Lord shall not prevent them which are asleep. For the Lord himself shall descend from heaven with a shout, with the voice of the archangel, and with the trump of God: and the dead in Christ shall rise first: Then we which are alive and remain shall be caught up together with them in the clouds, to meet the Lord in the air: and so shall we ever be with the Lord. Wherefore comfort one another with these words.

Faith

Jeffrey Pierson - January, 2010

Hebrews 11:1 (KJV)

Now faith is the substance of things hoped for, the evidence of things not seen.

When I was young I always heard this Scripture taught with an emphasis on the second half: "the evidence of things not seen." However, this literal 'half-truth' over time grew into a great lie in the church I was raised in. The belief became - absolute faith was merely waiting on God's promises because if you took any action yourself you didn't believe God would supply. I always had trouble with my faith because I felt a need to intervene but I KNEW I should not.

About six years ago I had a dream that I would have a son of my own flesh and blood. That dream has since been my evidence from Hebrews 11:1, yet I found my faith weak when around a year later my wife decided she didn't want to ever get pregnant. Then I found another Scripture that destroyed my old 'faith' entirely.

James 2:14-18 (KJV)

What doth it profit, my brethren, though a man say he hath faith, and have not works? can faith save him? If a brother or sister be naked, and destitute of daily food, And one of you say unto them, Depart in peace, be ye warmed and filled; notwithstanding ye give them not those things which are needful to the body; what doth it profit? Even so faith, if it hath not works, is dead, being alone. Yea, a man may say, Thou hast faith, and I have works: show me thy faith without thy works, and I will show thee my faith by my works.

I found this very troubling since I could do nothing to change her mind so I prayed for a solution to this dilemma. God's answer was for Sally to agree to reconsider when our credit cards were paid off. For a while I saw no progress,

then one day I noticed the bill in my hand was less than the one the month before. I now know what James meant by dead faith - until that moment my son was dead to me even though I tried to believe but when I saw my efforts were producing something, I knew God's promise would be fulfilled despite the fact that paying bills has nothing to do with having a son.

Since then whenever I doubted that my son would be born I would fall back into my 'works' of paying on credit cards. That became the 'substance'; something solid to hold onto and in time God proved his faithfulness by changing Sally's mind. I often wonder how many other Christians have fallen into the same trap the devil has made out of God's wisdom in Hebrews and find themselves questioning their faith after years of sitting and waiting, simply because they have been told a lie about the nature of faith.

If you find yourself weak in faith, look for the work God placed with his promise.

Sometimes it seems very reasonable; like saving money when He promised a house. Other times it makes no sense. Like being told that getting a job loading planes for $9.50 an hour will get you to a place where you can support your family and sometimes it seems contrary to your goal; as when God asks you to give away money in order to increase your finances. Whatever God asks you to do, if you do it, He will do as He has promised.

Thoughts on Love

Jeffrey Pierson - 2010

I remember when I was little I would look at my grandmother and I thought she had more love than anyone else. She always treated everyone like family and I can only remember a couple of times that she yelled at anyone.

As a teenager I believed I was incapable of that kind of love. For many people, myself included, love was a feeling, an emotion. I don't know entirely why but I have never felt a lot for people and as I grew into a teen I cared less and less for them until I had no concern for anyone but my immediate family beyond how they could be used for my gain. I began to grieve for the lost dream of being like my grandmother.

One day I heard a pastor teaching on love from 1 Corinthians 13.

1 Corinthians 13:4-7 (KJV2000)

Love suffers long, and is kind; love envies not; love vaunts not itself, is not puffed up, Does not behave itself rudely, seeks not her own, is not easily provoked, keeps no record of evil; Rejoices not in iniquity, but rejoices in the truth; Bears all things, believes all things, hopes all things, endures all things.

As I read these words I realized that the love in the Bible was not the feeling I had seemingly lost. Quite the contrary, true Godly love is treating people right even when you don't feel like it.

Even with this knowledge it still took me years to understand what it really means to love unconditionally. Later, as an adult, I sat on my grandmother's couch and listened to her as she wept in her room. Her husband whom she had promised to love until death had left her while she was sick and growing weaker every month. For her, there were no more kind, happy feelings for my grandfather but she did

not hate him. I heard, through her tears, the prayer of a wife for her husband's salvation. I can imagine no greater betrayal than what he did and no one more justified to "fall out of love" yet she still loved him.

My greatest desire is no longer to feel like she did for every one she met, for I know that feelings do not represent real love. I now long only to treat everyone I meet the way she treated my grandfather in her last days.

Named By God

Jeffrey Pierson - January, 2007

My father has four brothers and two sisters and every one of them has children. One has grandchildren. The last time I visited my grandmother she was buying presents for upwards of forty direct descendants. As they are by no means rich in the monetary sense, my grandparents were forced to be sparing with Christmas presents. We usually received a couple of small toys, generally bought in bulk, five or ten dollars for each one and a small gift that while not always unique managed to express her special love and recognition of each grandchild.

One year I received a gift from them that I can honestly say changed my life. It seemed simple enough, a small card with my name printed in calligraphy across the top and a brief paragraph explaining the origins of the name. I never forgot that moment. I cannot remember all that was printed on the card, but two words

have remained in my mind; "God's Peace".

Shortly thereafter my curiosity got the better of me and I asked my mother why I was named Jeffrey. Her response disappointed me at the time. She told me that on the way to the hospital my name just came to her and felt right. It seemed so meaningless to me for many years.

Like many church kids, I backslid during high school and the first year of college. I didn't truly return to God until six years ago, just after I got married. With the return of my faith came my fascination with my name and the names of family came shortly thereafter.

I studied the origins of my name over the years, and the more I studied this - and the Bible - several verses began to resonate within my mind.

Genesis 17:5 (KJV)

Neither shall thy name any more be called Abram, but thy name shall be Abraham; for a father of many nations have I made thee.

Genesis 32:28 (KJV)

And he said, Thy name shall be called no more Jacob, but Israel: for as a prince hast thou power with God and with men, and hast prevailed.

Matthew 16:17-18

And Jesus answered and said unto him, Blessed art thou, Simon Bar-jona: for flesh and blood hath not revealed it unto thee, but my Father which is in heaven. And I say also unto thee, That thou art Peter, and upon this rock I will build my church; and the gates of hell shall not prevail against it.

As I dwelt on these verses I realized that I was not the only one to be concerned with the meaning of names. God changed "high father" (Abram) to "father of a great multitude" (Abraham), "Supplanter" (Jacob) to "who prevails with God" (Israel), and "one who obeys" (Simon) had his name expanded to "one who obeys the rock" (Simon Peter). Two thousand years later he whispered a name in the ear of an expecting mother; Jeffrey Lee Pierson, "lion of God's Peace from the house of Peter".

I still strive every day to live up to that name and I fear that I still don't know the entire story that God spoke into that name. Yet every name that I have studied has shown a true picture of the person. My mother is the most methodic person I know and her advice has never failed me. Her name means "fountain of orderly words". My father is kind and quick to make friends and always ready to defend the weak. His name means "beloved lion". And my wife who, through all trials, falls into the arms of God brimming with

love for him. Her name means "bound to the savior".

And greatest of all Jesus means "Savior". He was also called Emmanuel which means "God with us".

Darrell L Pierson

Psalm 37:23 (KJV)

The steps of a good man are ordered by the LORD: and he delighteth in his way.

Thoughts about God

By Darrell Pierson

Watch and guide my steps, my Lord. Guide me in the way that I should go. Don't allow me, by poor discernment or bad judgment, to do things that are stupid. My desire, God, is to please you, to enjoy this life and show others how to do the same. My greatest pleasure comes from Your presence. Allow me the good pleasure of finding You always near. To share my belief with others can only be accomplished by Your Word and applying it in a proper manner. To see You work in the lives of those around me is always wonderful. And to look back at what You have done in my life amazes me. I never saw it coming. Thank you lord for all the changes You have made and want to make in my life.

I want to make my best effort to perform all that You have for me to accomplish in this life. Thank you for all the wonderful things on this earth. They each point out Your greatness and brings pleasure to my

spirit. All these things remind me that You were, You are, and You are to come.

When I look into the vastness of the sky, I see You. When I look into things magnified to make them visible again, I see You. How can a right thinking Man say, "There is no God". Thank you, God, that I can perceive You as a mighty Friend who has made a great sacrifice to allow me the awesome pleasure of an intimate relationship with You, by way of Christ, Your Word, and the Holy Ghost. I would feel like a beggar and forever indebted to You, eccept that Christ has paid the price. Never let me waste any of what You freely give to me.

Your Servant

Darrell

Boots

I've noticed since I moved to Texas that the men with trucks have a habit of sticking their boots behind the rear window of their truck between the cab and the bed. I often take a second look because the initial reaction is a concern that someone is stuck in an awkward position. And then I remember they are just boots to be stored there until they are needed. Boots remind me of my father.

Have you ever looked at a pair of boots? Well-worn boots are often scuffed and dirty. As a child, my father would often come home tired from a long day on his feet and ask one of us girls to remove his boots. We would struggle with the shoe strings and eventually wrestle the dirty, smelly boots off his feet. I never liked the task.

As a child, I saw those dirty boots as a job that I had to do because my father was too tired to take his boots off. Today I look at boots quite differently.

My husband's job also requires him to wear boots but he has never ask me to remove them. It was my husband that taught me to appreciate boots.

Most evenings my husband would take his dirty, worn out boots and polish them to look the best they could. He took pains to ensure they were clean and presentable. Sometimes he would struggle with the broken laces, trying to make them reach far enough to secure a knot for a few more weeks until we had the money to buy new ones. There were times that his boots were falling apart to the point that we would need to take a trip to a discount store where he would buy the cheapest he could find, even though a few more dollars would have given him a great deal more comfort. There were many days those boots would take him on long trips away from home, working long hours to earn enough to pay the bills.

A simple pair of boots but they bring to mind a lifetime of memories. It's not the boots that matter but the man who wears them. My husband's boots taught me that there is no price too great to pay, nor any load too heavy to bear, when you're doing it for those you love.

Today, when I see a pair of boots, I don't just remember my father and the uncomfortable task of removing his boots. Instead I am humbled by the man who taught me the price paid by the one who willingly wears them.

1 Thessalonians 4:11-12 (NLT)

Make it your goal to live a quiet life, minding your own business and working with your hands, just as we instructed you before. Then people who are not Christians will respect the way you live, and you will not need to depend on others.

Mowing the Lawn

Matthew 25:23 (NASV)

"His master said to him, 'Well done, good and faithful slave. You were faithful with a few things, I will put you in charge of many things; enter into the joy of your master.'

There will come a time when each of us will find ourselves face to face with our Lord and when we do, we want to hear those words *'good and faithful servant'*. **Matthew 25:34-40** gives us the definition of a faithful servant. As I read thru this description I caught a glimpse of an individual who is selfless and giving. One who cares for others and sacrifices his own needs in exchange for meeting someone else's. I see my husband.

My husband is a faithful man - I've often compared him to "Peter" in Jesus' day. He stands out as zealous, boisterous and forever the giver.

Raised in the country, Darrell loves the outdoors and flowers are his passion. He cares for the lawn and he loves to just be in the middle of God's creation. Back home in West Virginia we had several acres to tend but here we have only a small lot so Darrell has developed a habit of mowing the lawns of empty houses and needy neighbors.

One day last summer we received the 'dreaded' letter from our Home Owners Association stating that our lawn was not up to par. They had confused us with the house just down the street that carries the same house number. For Darrell, however, it was the greatest insult. Monday morning he called the Association and vehemently attacked their intelligence, proclaiming that he was the man who not only mowed his lawn but also every empty house on the block and some of our friends' lawns as well. The dear lady apologized and agreed to withdraw the complaint and then meekly ask if he would consider mowing the yard of a terminally ill man a

few streets over. Taken off guard, he gladly agreed.

For the next few months Darrell went by the old man's house each week to groom his yard, never troubling him, but quietly doing the mundane tasks of lawn care. One day in early winter Darrell went to make one final pass thru the yard before the cold weather took over and a neighbor stopped by to say hello. Darrell asked how the old man was doing. The neighbor responded that the man had passed away a couple of months before. In his usual good humor, Darrell put the situation in perspective and chose to believe that God and that dear old man had a good laugh watching from heaven as he mowed the lawn week after week for someone who had already departed this earth. God's instruction to us has always been to remain faithful and Darrell was indeed faithful.

Matthew 25:34-40 (NIV)

"Then the King will say to those on his right, 'Come, you who are blessed by my Father; take your inheritance, the kingdom prepared for you since the creation of the world. For I was hungry and you gave me something to eat, I was thirsty and you gave me something to drink, I was a stranger and you invited me in, I needed clothes and you clothed me, I was sick and you looked after me, I was in prison and you came to visit me.'

"Then the righteous will answer him, 'Lord, when did we see you hungry and feed you, or thirsty and give you something to drink? When did we see you a stranger and invite you in, or needing clothes and clothe you? When did we see you sick or in prison and go to visit you?'

"The King will reply, 'Truly I tell you, whatever you did for one of the least of these brothers and sisters of mine, you did for me.'

Teach

Deuteronomy 32:2 (NLT)

Let my teaching fall on you like rain; let my speech settle like dew. Let my words fall like rain on tender grass, like gentle showers on young plants.

Where am I going?

Have you ever had an epiphany? A sudden and completely life altering thought that redraws your life's roadmap? I had one of those moments a few years ago. I considered how I spent my life, learning to be a better person, studying the word, increasing knowledge, gaining wisdom and understanding. My whole life was wrapped up in improving, growing, reaching beyond what I am and what I know. Then, when I finaly think I have 'figured it out', I'll die.

This, as all train rides do, lead me to other ponderings. Why go through all the trouble to learn all this 'stuff' and then leave? All that I have gained will mean nothing as I spend eternity in blissful ease.

Later, I ended my reflection by determining that life isn't over when we leave here, it is a continuum – this life is just our child days. We become adults on the other side of what we call 'death.'

In all my 'ponderings', as silly as they may seem, I have grown to believe that life is full of learning and learning is our preparation for teaching and teaching is my passion. Somewhere on the other side of death, I hope I will continue to teach – I don't know who, I don't know what, I don't even know why, but, oh how I love to teach.

Ephesians 4:11-13 (NLT)

Now these are the gifts Christ gave to the church: the apostles, the prophets, the evangelists, and the pastors and teachers. Their responsibility is to equip God's people to do his work and build up the church, the body of Christ. This will continue until we all come to such unity in our faith and knowledge of God's Son that we will be mature in the Lord, measuring up to the full and complete standard of Christ.

An Opened Door

Revelations 3:8a (NLT)

"I know all the things you do, and I have opened a door for you that no one can close."

An open door is an opportunity and God places them in our lives every day. They can take on the form of a friend in need of encouragement, a parent who is lonely, a child needing a mentor, or it can look like a new job, a better home, or a trip across the globe.

Many times we fail to recognize opportunities God puts in our path because they aren't what we would choose to do or they require more of us than we are willing to give. We ignore them, hoping that something more attractive will come along.

The open door God provides, however, is a reward for the life we are living. What lies beyond that door reflects the true heart of God.

A Just and Merciful God

I was raised in a church that taught us that God was just and He would always punish even the smallest sin. I can remember pastors teaching that every day something would happen to cause us to sin; we would stub our toe and curse in pain, get cut off in traffic and shout in a hateful rage, or we may see someone with possessions beyond our humble financial means and we may covet it. He then insisted that every day after repenting of any sins we remembered we must ask God to forgive us of any sins we had forgotten or were unaware of. To this day, if I am tired and not careful, I fill my prayers with "Father forgive me."

Later I learned about pastors who taught of a loving and merciful God who would forgive all your sins because He wanted us to go to heaven, whether we ask Him to or not. I saw their congregations walk in constant sin, believing that even if they died in the act of sinning, God's grace would cover their un-repented sins.

It was years before I could accept that both of these opposing views were the broken remains of the true Gospel that points us to the character and nature of a just *AND* merciful God. I found that God would hold me accountable for my sins and yet gladly forgive me when I ask. And I found that sin is a willful choice to disobey God, not a fumbled misstep that we aren't even aware of.

God not only forgives my sins when I ask but He helps me to live a holy life; not on my own but through His Spirit. Because He is Holy and died on a cross, I can be righteous and Holy, cleansed by His blood.

Romans 6:1-2 (NIV)

What shall we say, then? Shall we go on sinning so that grace may increase? By no means! We are those who have died to sin; how can we live in it any longer?

1 Peter 1:13-16 (NIV)

Therefore, with minds that are alert and fully sober, set your hope on the grace to be brought to you when Jesus Christ is revealed at His coming. As obedient children, do not conform to the evil desires you had when you lived in ignorance. But just as He who called you is holy, so be holy in all you do; for it is written: "Be holy, because I am holy."

Revelation

As a child, I developed a love for the language of the King James Version and even today I find comfort in its Old English rhythm. A lifetime of reading, however, does not provide me with the understanding of what God is telling me in His Word. It can only come through divine revelation by the Spirit of God.

1 Corinthians 2:14 (NIV)

The person without the Spirit does not accept the things that come from the Spirit of God but considers them foolishness, and cannot understand them because they are discerned only through the Spirit.

In all my years of learning, I still find that when I open God's Word, there is the opportunity for new revelation, words of encouragement, and lessons for life. I have barely touched the surface of the knowledge that it holds, but I am

confident it will awaken in God's perfect time.

1 Corinthians 2:9b-10 (NLT)

"No eye has seen, no ear has heard, and no mind has imagined what God has prepared for those who love Him." But it was to us that God revealed these things by His Spirit. For His Spirit searches out everything and shows us God's deep secrets.

Not Just For Abraham

One of my greatest mistakes has been to overlook God's promises simply because they were given first to Abraham. However, when I looked closely at the Scriptures I find that God is unchangeable and His promises are eternal to all that love and obey His word.

Abraham was given a promise that he would be a father and from his son a nation would be born that would have the responsibility of teaching God's laws to the entire world. They would be the channel God used to bless all the nations of the world, providing redemption through the Messiah and establishing the Kingdom of God.

This nation became known as Israel. However, when Jesus entered the picture, many Israelites rejected Him. God then adopted a new people to become heirs of Abraham's promise and they were given the responsibility of teaching the World about the Kingdom of God. These people are known as Christians.

Ephesians 3:6 (NLT)

And this is God's plan: Both Gentiles and Jews who believe the Good News share equally in the riches inherited by God's children. Both are part of the same body, and both enjoy the promise of blessings because they belong to Christ Jesus.

A New Year

On the morning of this new, fresh year, I reflect on my life in Christ and take a personal, fresh look at how I really feel about my Lord.

Do I really Love God? What must I do to show that I love Him...

1 Corinthians 13:1-13 (NIV)

If I speak in the tongues of men or of angels, but do not have love, I am only a resounding gong or a clanging cymbal. If I have the gift of prophecy and can fathom all mysteries and all knowledge, and if I have a faith that can move mountains, but do not have love, I am nothing. If I give all I possess to the poor and give over my body to hardship that I may boast, but do not have love, I gain nothing.

Love is patient

- I will be patient with God, He does not always reveal His plan to me, but I will love and trust Him.

Love is kind

- I will be kind to God, I will not confront, blame, or challenge Him in any way,

It does not envy

- I will not envy God's power and position, resenting that I cannot do what only He can.

It does not boast

- I will not boast of the favor God has shown me.

It is not proud

- I will not be proud, for I know who I am and I am grateful that He has not discarded me.

It does not dishonor others

- I will not dishonor Him but seek to obey and reflect His very character and nature in everything I say and do.

It is not self-seeking

- I will not seek to please or benefit myself, making decisions based on what I want or think is good. It is not about what I want but about what God wants for me and I accept that He knows all that I have need of.

It is not easily angered

- I will not easily be angered when the circumstances of my life do not reflect my understanding of God but I will seek to understand Him more and trust Him through every situation.

It keeps no record of wrongs

- I will not keep a record of perceived wrongs, things that I felt should have been different but weren't. Situations that I wanted Him to intervene in, knowing He had a better plan. I will

instead walk on - and thank Him for His sovereign reign in my life. I will allow Him to reign. I will not keep a list of how I would have done it differently.

Love does not delight in evil but rejoices with the truth.

- I will take no pleasure in sin and injustices – for I cannot understand them, nor do I wish to give them glory, but I will rejoice in the undeniable truth that is God's alone – this truth will be fully revealed at a later time in its entirety. I need only delight in its existence and embrace the portion that He has revealed to me.

It always protects, always trusts, always hopes, always perseveres.

- I will protect my relationship with My God. I will always trust Him. I will always hope in Him. I will always stand my ground - because He will grant me the power to do so.

Love never fails.

- My love for my God will never bow to doubts and fears or the influences of others, for my love is stable, founded in who He is and not who I am.

But where there are prophecies, they will cease

- When there are those who reveal promises of tomorrow, I will remember these promises will someday become of no importance - for tomorrow will become yesterday;

Where there are tongues, they will be stilled

- When there are those who give me words of hope and encouragement, I will remember there will be a day when that hope and encouragement will become silent for they will no longer be required. Our hope will be fully achieved.

Where there is knowledge, it will pass away

- When there are those who share their firsthand knowledge and experience, I will remember that there is coming a day when such knowledge and experience will no longer have a bearing - for I accept that all things have not yet been revealed but when they are revealed our current knowledge will be inadequate.

For we know in part and we prophesy in part, but when completeness comes, what is in part disappears.

- For I know only a part of God's plan and purpose, and prophesy can only reflect what is revealed to me today. However, when the fullness of all things come to pass, these things that are only partial and incomplete will disappear.

When I was a child, I talked like a child, I thought like a child, I reasoned like a child. When I became a man, I put the ways of childhood behind me.

For now we see only a reflection as in a mirror; then we shall see face to face.

- I accept that I see only a reflection, as if I were looking in a mirror, of all that My God is and does. But not too far in the future I will see My God face to face.

Now I know in part; then I shall know fully, even as I am fully known.

- Today I know only what He has allowed me to know about Him. Then I shall know Him in His fullness and glory and I understand that He already knows me in my completeness, which includes all my perfect and imperfect nature and acts.

And now these three remain: faith, hope and love

- There are three important expressions of my life in Christ: faith in God, hope in all He has promised and love for Him, just as He described in His word.

But the greatest of these is love

- But the greatest of these expressions is to love the Lord My God with all my heart, soul, mind and body and to love my neighbors the same way.

1 John 4:20-21 (NIV)

Whoever claims to love God yet hates a brother or sister is a liar. For whoever does not love their brother and sister, whom they have seen, cannot love God, whom they have not seen. And He has given us this command: Anyone who loves God must also love their brother and sister.

All Will Know...

I read the promises in God's Word and know they were meant for me. The promises of health, a long life, prosperity, the promise to "speak to my mountain" yet when I lift up my head from God's Word I wonder, "What am I doing wrong?"

Jesus taught us never to doubt God's Word and I have lived my life by that principle. I refuse to believe there is any error in Scripture. If it's written in the Bible, it is the only truth. The dilemma I face is when I am doing all I know to do and yet my life doesn't fit the picture I see inside of those pages.

Lately I've looked into the eyes of my struggling family and friends and wondered, "What can I say to encourage them in the middle of their reality? What would make their journey a little easier and restore their hope?"

I can't tell you why there are times our reality seems to contradict God's promises. I won't attempt to belittle our

struggles. But I will say this; we can't give up. God's Word is our only true reality. We must hold on to each promise with all the stubbornness we can muster. There will come a day when we will know, WE WIN.

Malachi 3:13-18 (NIV)

"You have spoken arrogantly against me," says the Lord. "Yet you ask, 'What have we said against you?'

"You have said, 'It is futile to serve God. What do we gain by carrying out his requirements and going about like mourners before the Lord Almighty? But now we call the arrogant blessed. Certainly evildoers prosper, and even when they put God to the test, they get away with it.' "

Then those who feared the Lord talked with each other, and the Lord listened and heard. A scroll of remembrance was written in his presence concerning those who

feared the Lord and honored his name.

"On the day when I act," says the Lord Almighty, "they will be my treasured possession. I will spare them, just as a father has compassion and spares his son who serves him. And you will again see the distinction between the righteous and the wicked, between those who serve God and those who do not.

Sowing and Reaping

The law of sowing and reaping is a universal law, just like gravity. These laws were written in the beginning of time and are not governed by righteousness or evil. They cannot be manipulated for our own benefit, nor will they change as long as the earth remains.

Across the world you will hear the message of sowing and reaping. Unfortunately the message is often rooted in greed and filled with misinformation. Many of us have developed a dislike for the principal simply because we have glimpsed someone's darker intent.

Among the overwhelming multitude of voices, however, if we listen closely we will find the glorious truth that God proclaimed over 6,000 years ago ....whatever you sow, you will reap.

Galatians 6:7-10

Do not be deceived: God is not mocked, for whatever one sows, that will he also reap. For the one who sows to his own flesh will from the flesh reap corruption, but the one who sows to the Spirit will from the Spirit reap eternal life. And let us not grow weary of doing good, for in due season we will reap, if we do not give up. So then, as we have opportunity, let us do good to everyone, and especially to those who are of the household of faith.

Moments to Remember

Psalm 78:1-7 (NLT)

O my people, listen to my instructions. Open your ears to what I am saying, for I will speak to you in a parable. I will teach you hidden lessons from our past—stories we have heard and known, stories our ancestors handed down to us. We will not hide these truths from our children; we will tell the next generation about the glorious deeds of the LORD, about his power and his mighty wonders. For he issued his laws to Jacob; he gave his instructions to Israel. He commanded our ancestors to teach them to their children, so the next generation might know them—even the children not yet born—and they in turn will teach their own children. So each generation should set its hope anew on God, not forgetting his glorious miracles and obeying his commands.

Angie - August 10, 2008

To my daughter, Angie, who I love more than life.

The Lord assured me this week you would be coming home, whole and complete, healed emotionally and spiritually. There is a ministry for you. I am anxious for you to be home again. I look forward to meeting the man who will be your husband. You both will be active in ministry.

Every day I ask the Lord to do the following for you.

Every day, when you wake up, I ask that He will be the first thing on your mind. That you will remember your relationship with him and long for it to be restored and that your faith will be healed.

Your future husband will have a heart toward the Lord. You both will be ministers of the gospel and an active part of mission work. You will have a little girl someday. I don't know if she will be adopted or not.

Have faith, baby girl, God has everything under control.

I love you. Mom

She came home in the fall of 2009. Today she has a wonderful Christian husband and 4 wonderful children, one of which is a beautiful little girl.

Christmas

I've never read anything about America in the Bible. But the concept of a nation under God is there, just as the concept of giving is...the very principles we learn through the story of St. Nickolas.

It is sad that so many people misunderstand the story of Santa, having no clue what or how a man that gave gifts to others could be a positive example of God's love for us.

Many have said, "I think it is lying to my children" and yet they continue to encourage them to pretend to be Captain America, GI Joe, Cinderella, or even play Mommy and Daddy. They will embrace their make believe play through movies, video games, and story time, and yet they call it lies to teach a real life lesson through a parable of gift giving during the Christmas season.

My parents allowed me to believe in Santa but they never lied to me. They relayed to me an exciting story of a man

who lovingly gave gifts at Christmas and they allowed me to pretend play that he would visit me too. They never said - there is a Santa, they simply let me dream. I have not been scarred by those dreams. I look back on them with fond memories and today I truly understand that the celebration of Christmas is about Christ coming into this world to give gifts to men and I learned some of the ways I can imitate Christ is through the parable of St. Nick.

I challenge all who read this to 'play' Santa this Christmas; not from the receiving side but the giving side. Give a gift to someone this year - someone who can't possibly give back to you. Maybe even give it in secret. Give them the joy of receiving something free - with no strings attached and no person they must feel indebted to. Teach them a lesson they will never forget. Teach them that there is still alive today the spirit of giving, the spirit embraced by the story of Santa Clause. After all, isn't that what happens on Christmas morning for all the children

who believe in Santa Clause? They receive from a secret giver something that they can never repay. They don't know who it is, so they call him Santa. Someday perhaps they too, will be gift givers, expecting nothing in return but giving just for the joy of giving.

2 Corinthians 9:6 (NIV)

Remember this: Whoever sows sparingly will also reap sparingly, and whoever sows generously will also reap generously.

My Comfort Zone

It had been a difficult four years. Mom's terminal illness, Dad's betrayal, our internal struggles. We were traveling 150 miles round trip to church and wondering why.

Darrell loved the country and the farm. He was determined to retire there. I had a good job and so did he. We'd be set. Just a few more years.

Then one day while I was sitting in my office, Darrell walks in and sets down across from me.

"How would you like to be moved out of your comfort zone?"

His company was shutting down and they offered him the opportunity to go to Canada, Kentucky, or Texas. The choice was ours. Or we could stay where we were and trust God would find him another job. But there was something going on in Texas and God wanted us there.

As we packed up our world and headed for a new one, I thanked God for the adventure we were about to undertake. But with all adventures come new tests and trials. The days ahead were a mystery. Little did we know we were starting the greatest journey of our lives.

James 4:13-15 (NASV)

Come now, you who say, "Today or tomorrow we will go to such and such a city, and spend a year there and engage in business and make a profit." Yet you do not know what your life will be like tomorrow. You are just a vapor that appears for a little while and then vanishes away. Instead, you ought to say, "If the Lord wills, we will live and also do this or that."

The Water Walker

I've always loved the Bible story of Peter walking on water. I've envisioned him stepping out of a boat and moving across the water while his fellow disciples stood back. Watching, they must have been surprised at his courage as he did what none of them dare try. Through the years I've heard messages of Peter taking his eyes off Jesus and beginning to sink, of how he cried out and was pulled up from the grasp of the sea into the safety of his master's arms. I longed to be the kind of person who had the courage to step out onto the water, daring to do the unthinkable .... Trusting .... Believing .... Water walking.

A while back, Darrell wrestled with a life changing decision. Although we prayed, a clear answer didn't come. It would have been a relief to hear the Lord say "Do this" or "Do that". Obedience is always easier when the commands we are given are clear. But Heaven remained silent.

Experience has taught me to listen to the still, quiet voice of the Lord and it was during this time that He spoke these words to me...

> *"There are few times in your life when you are granted an opportunity to walk on water, so walk."*

Those simple words set in place a chain of events that would catapult our lives into a new dimension. Awed, frightened and excited, we took the challenge and began the walk.

Within days our world began to crash around us. It felt like a whirlwind had hit. My head was spinning, my emotions were sweeping over me in waves, I was confused as I grasped for spiritual air, striving to keep from drowning in events I could not control. After weeks of distress I again heard the voice of my Lord ...

> *"Everyone wants to walk on water, but what they fail to realize is that when they step out of the boat,*

they've just stepped into the worst storm of their life."

The next 11 months were among the worst .... and the best ... times of our lives. We experienced a fatal car crash, my daughter left home, my father passed away, Darrell struggled with his health, insecurities, and overwhelming helplessness. Finances were strained. The truck broke down. Our first grandson was born and he and our daughter-n-law fought for their lives. My sister was healed. My daughter came home.

Again and again we experienced the hits, and the joys, that challenged and strengthened our faith. There were times we questioned our decision, times we were ready to call a halt and turn back. The struggle seemed greater than we could handle. Were we doing the right thing?

We labored, we sacrificed, and we fought discouragement, offenses and self-doubts as well as God doubts. And Heaven sat quiet.

We neared our breaking point, tired, discouraged and stretched as far as we could go. Confused, we couldn't understand why there was no answer to our prayers when we were so determined to build God's Kingdom. After months of silence I heard His voice again...

> *"If all I ask of you during this season is to learn to trust me, is it enough?"*

Could it be that everything we were facing had no other purpose than to teach us to trust God? If that were true, was that enough of a reason to continue on through the storm? I knew that we were headed to another level and that level required a greater trust than we had ever known. We NEEDED this time to prepare. New revelation came as the Lord whispered yet again;

> *"It was Peter I chose on Pentecost."*

Peter, the "Water Walker".

Gratefully I bowed my head in understanding. There came a day when Heaven needed a man who would preach

a message that had never been preached before. A man that would stand in front of a group of people that had never seen what they would see on that Pentecost morning. Heaven needed a "Water Walker" and Peter had the resume to fill the job.

With new insight I saw that our desire to be "Water Walkers" had allowed us to be a vessel, meet for the master's use.

Tonight we are coming to an end of a year of storms and a peace sweeps over my spirit. I do not know what our next season will bring but I know that we have done our best to ride the waves and to keep our eyes on Jesus. We've been faithful, we've tried to follow every directive God gave us. If we missed any mark, it wasn't intentional. It is in this knowledge that we can rest.

Then again I hear the Lord speak in His simple, direct way.

"You did it."

We walked on water ... we survived the storm.

With our shoulders a little straighter we praise God that we will be among those that bear the name "Water Walker". We'll no longer yearn to be like Peter, we are like Peter. As we stand ready to do what we have never done before, we anticipate a "Pentecostal" victory.

As we settle in, waiting for the next season of our life, we wonder if there is anything we should be doing. I am comforted as the Lord assures me once again.

"Just wait for the harvest."

Seedtime and Harvest

Genesis 8:22 (NIV)

"As long as the earth endures, seedtime and harvest, cold and heat, summer and winter, day and night will never cease."

2 Corinthians 9:6 (NIV)

Remember this: Whoever sows sparingly will also reap sparingly, and whoever sows generously will also reap generously.

Galatians 6:8 (NIV)

Whoever sows to please their flesh, from the flesh will reap destruction; whoever sows to please the Spirit, from the Spirit will reap eternal life.

Water of Life

John 7:37-38 (ESV)

...Jesus stood up and cried out, "If anyone thirsts, let him come to me and drink. Whoever believes in me, as the Scripture has said, 'Out of his heart will flow rivers of living water.'"

Some people do not like the taste of water – they will substitute their need for it with other things, such as tea, juice, pop or coffee. Many people do not like the 'taste' of Jesus, either; so they substitute other things to attempt to fill their need for a savior. Others, unknowingly, become dehydrated for lack of water just as many people become spiritually dry for lack of an active relationship with the Lord.

Then there are those who seem to bubble like a clear, beautiful brook, constant in their joy and strength. These are the ones who drink freely from the river of God and from deep within them flows the river of life that will never run dry.

Revelation 22:17 (NIV)

The Spirit and the bride say, "Come!" And let the one who hears say, "Come!" Let the one who is thirsty come; and let the one who wishes take the free gift of the water of life.

Thank You

John 3:14-16 (NIV)

Just as Moses lifted up the snake in the wilderness, so the Son of Man must be lifted up, that everyone who believes may have eternal life in Him." For God so loved the world that He gave His one and only Son, that whoever believes in Him shall not perish but have eternal life.

In the shadow of the Easter Holiday I was reminded of a time a few years ago when, during a communion service, I lifted my hands to honor and praise my Lord. Quietly I heard within my spirit a single sentence – *"You've never thanked me."* I find that when the Lord speaks to me, it doesn't involve lengthy lectures or explanations but just a single statement that is so profound, I am forever changed.

Having attended church all my life I have often thanked the Lord for what He was doing in my life – for those things He had done for me in the past but I could not

remember ever having said a simple "Thank You" for what He did on the Cross. With a repentant heart, I quietly told my savior a simple, heartfelt thanks. It seemed so insufficient, but at that moment, it was all He ask of me.

When was the last time you said "Thank You for the Cross?"

Your Reward

Have you ever come face to face with an undeniable need? Not the man that carries a sign standing by the side of the road waiting to run to the store for an alcohol fix - or the individual that's anxious to live an easy life while others pay their bills. These individuals have definite needs but we are not equipped to solve their problem. What we can do, however, is meet the very real needs of the individuals God places in our path. We can reach out to the neighbor whose home burned to the ground, or we can help buy groceries for a friend out of work.

We may never have crossed paths with someone that is truly in need but someday we will and what we do with that need defines who we are.

Matthew 6:1-4 (NASV)

"Beware of practicing your righteousness before men to be noticed by them; otherwise you have no reward with your Father who is in heaven. "So when you give to the poor, do not sound a trumpet before you, as the hypocrites do in the synagogues and in the streets, so that they may be honored by men. Truly I say to you, they have their reward in full. "But when you give to the poor, do not let your left hand know what your right hand is doing, so that your giving will be in secret; and your Father who sees what is done in secret will reward you.

The End of the Day

Psalm 39:4-5 (NLT)

"LORD, remind me how brief my time on earth will be. Remind me that my days are numbered—how fleeting my life is. You have made my life no longer than the width of my hand. My entire lifetime is just a moment to you; at best, each of us is but a breath."

The Trial

Job 16:19-21 (NIV)

Even now my witness is in heaven; my advocate is on high. My intercessor is my friend as my eyes pour out tears to God; on behalf of a man He pleads with God as one pleads for a friend.

When I read these three verses I am reminded of a lesson I learned many years ago.

There was a man who had a dream...

He dreamed he stood in a courtroom as one accused before his judge and prosecutor. Beside him was his attorney. As the prosecutor stepped forward, he began to quote the defendants own words, reciting declarations of healing, victory, commitment and righteousness. The man heard the prosecutor refer to a Sunday School Class he had taught concerning the salvation we experience thru the blood of Jesus Christ. Time and again he repeated statements the man

had proclaimed throughout his life. Statements of Love, Hope, Joy and Peace.

Then the prosecutor began to accuse the defendant. He reminded the court of the days the defendant walked in sickness, despite his proclamations of healing. He spoke of the days of dark doubt the defendant had tried so desperately to hide from those brothers and sisters in Christ that he wanted to encourage. He ridiculed the man for his belief that he was 'saved' when he had many times walked in failure. As the courtroom fell silent, the defendants' lawyer stepped forward. His defense was a simple statement.

Romans 8:1-2 (NIV)

Therefore, there is now no condemnation for those who are in Christ Jesus, because through Christ Jesus the law of the Spirit who gives life has set you free from the law of sin and death.

Romans 4:7-8 (NASV)

"Blessed are those whose lawless deeds have been forgiven, and whose sins have been covered; blessed is the man whose sin the Lord will not take into account."

The Other Side of Here

There has been a lot of talk lately about what people would do if they only had a few days left to live. What would they say, what would be most important to them. People have at times written their own eulogy in an effort to make a final statement to the world. My message to you is simple:

Be There!

Revelation 21:1-4 (KJV)

And I saw a new heaven and a new earth: for the first heaven and the first earth were passed away; and there was no more sea. And I John saw the holy city, New Jerusalem, coming down from God out of heaven, prepared as a bride adorned for her husband. And I heard a great voice out of heaven saying, Behold, the tabernacle of God is with men, and He will dwell with them, and they shall be His people, and God Himself shall be with them, and be their God. And God shall wipe away all tears from their eyes; and there shall be no more death, neither sorrow, nor crying, neither shall there be any more pain: for the former things are passed away.

Rest

Revelations 21:4-5 (NLT)

He will wipe every tear from their eyes, and there will be no more death or sorrow or crying or pain. All these things are gone forever." And the one sitting on the throne said, "Look, I am making everything new!" And then He said to me, "Write this down, for what I tell you is trustworthy and true."

There have been many times I've longed for the day when this Scripture would be fulfilled. I've imagined what it would be like to never suffer pain, worry, loss or even death.

While God promises we will have all this when we reach heaven, He does not tell us we are free from struggles here on earth. If we live and breathe - we will see trouble. The secret is, what will we do with the trouble?

Matthew 11:28-30 (NLT)

Then Jesus said, "Come to me, all of you who are weary and carry heavy burdens, and I will give you rest. Take my yoke upon you. Let me teach you, because I am humble and gentle at heart, and you will find rest for your souls. For my yoke is easy to bear, and the burden I give you is light."

Heaven's Mystery

A few years ago I had an unexpected dream just before our grandson, David, was born. I dreamed that my long departed granddad brought me little baby David. He was so gentle and smiled ever so slightly. In the dream I knew David had been loved and welcomed into our family and granddad was the one who was assign to escort David to us and charge us with his care. I have often thought that there was something I didn't fully understand, but I had received a glimmer of something so very precious.

A few years later, my son-n-law had a dream before his daughter, Kearney, was born. He dreamed that my mother brought her to him.

This all seemed so remarkable but then there was more.

Just the other day, little two year old Kearney was looking at my mother's picture on the wall. She told her mom, "That's my heaven grandma". Angie,

surprised, tried not to confuse Kearney, so she simply replied, "She is?" Kearney said, "Yea, she laughs a lot." Kearney then told Angie that mom had held her until Angie came to get her.

I think there are things we still don't fully understand.

Psalm 139:15-18 (NLT)

You watched me as I was being formed in utter seclusion, as I was woven together in the dark of the womb. You saw me before I was born. Every day of my life was recorded in your book. Every moment was laid out before a single day had passed. How precious are your thoughts about me, O God. They cannot be numbered! I can't even count them; they outnumber the grains of sand! And when I wake up, you are still with me!

The Lamb Of God

Genesis 22:7-8 (NIV)

Isaac spoke to Abraham his father and said, "My father!" And he said, "Here I am, my son." And he said, "Behold, the fire and the wood, but where is the lamb for the burnt offering?" Abraham said, "God will provide for Himself the lamb for the burnt offering, my son." So the two of them walked on together.

I'm often humbled by the exchange between Abraham and Isaac. I have the advantage of hindsight. They had the extraordinary faith that would mark their place in history. While I look back with thankfulness, they looked forward with anticipation. Each of us look to the Lamb, Jesus Christ, the ultimate sacrifice for their sins and mine and the source of help for a desperate world.

Each New Year is one in which we find ourselves in a unique position of looking back and forward. We remember the year

we've lived thru, the good and the bad and we anticipate the coming year. For most of us we have dreams, hopes, and plans for this upcoming year. Some of us experience anxiety at the unknown and others foresee a future shadowed by dark clouds. During this season, whatever we see behind us or imagine before us, let us not forget to take a good look at the Lamb. He is forever the source of help for our desperate world.

John 1:29 (KJV)

....John saw Jesus coming toward him and said, "Look, the Lamb of God who takes away the sin of the world!

To God Be the Glory

Psalm 118:23 (ESV)

This is the LORD's doing; it is marvelous in our eyes.

Tonight it is quiet in the house. Darrell is working at the church and I've done all I can for those that God placed on my heart today. I sit here and I look back over the events of these past few weeks and I am once more awed at what my Lord has done. He is awesome in all His doings and I am humbled that He loves me and has included me in His Kingdom.

Jude 1:24-25 (NLT)

Now all glory to God, who is able to keep you from falling away and will bring you with great joy into His glorious presence without a single fault. All glory to Him who alone is God, our Savior through Jesus Christ our Lord. All glory, majesty, power, and authority are His before all time, and in the present, and beyond all time! Amen.

www.ingramcontent.com/pod-product-compliance
Lightning Source LLC
Chambersburg PA
CBHW022353040426
42450CB00005B/168